MY FIRST BIG BOOK OF COLORING

Dinosaurs

56 images

ORNITISCHIANS AND SAURISCHIANS

Kh. EL.

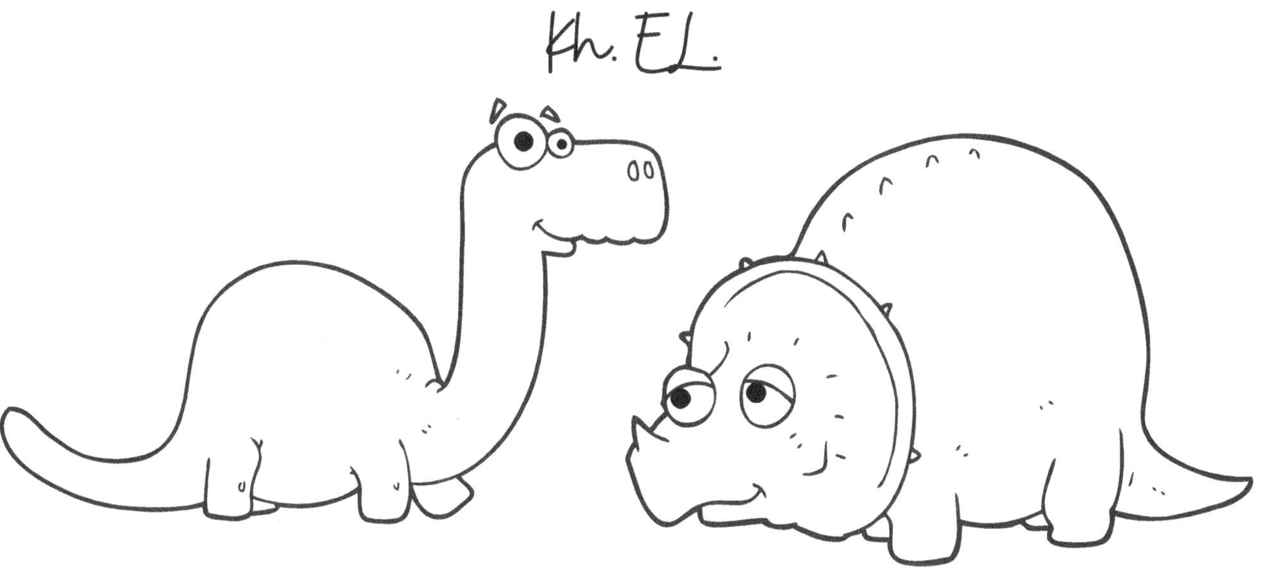

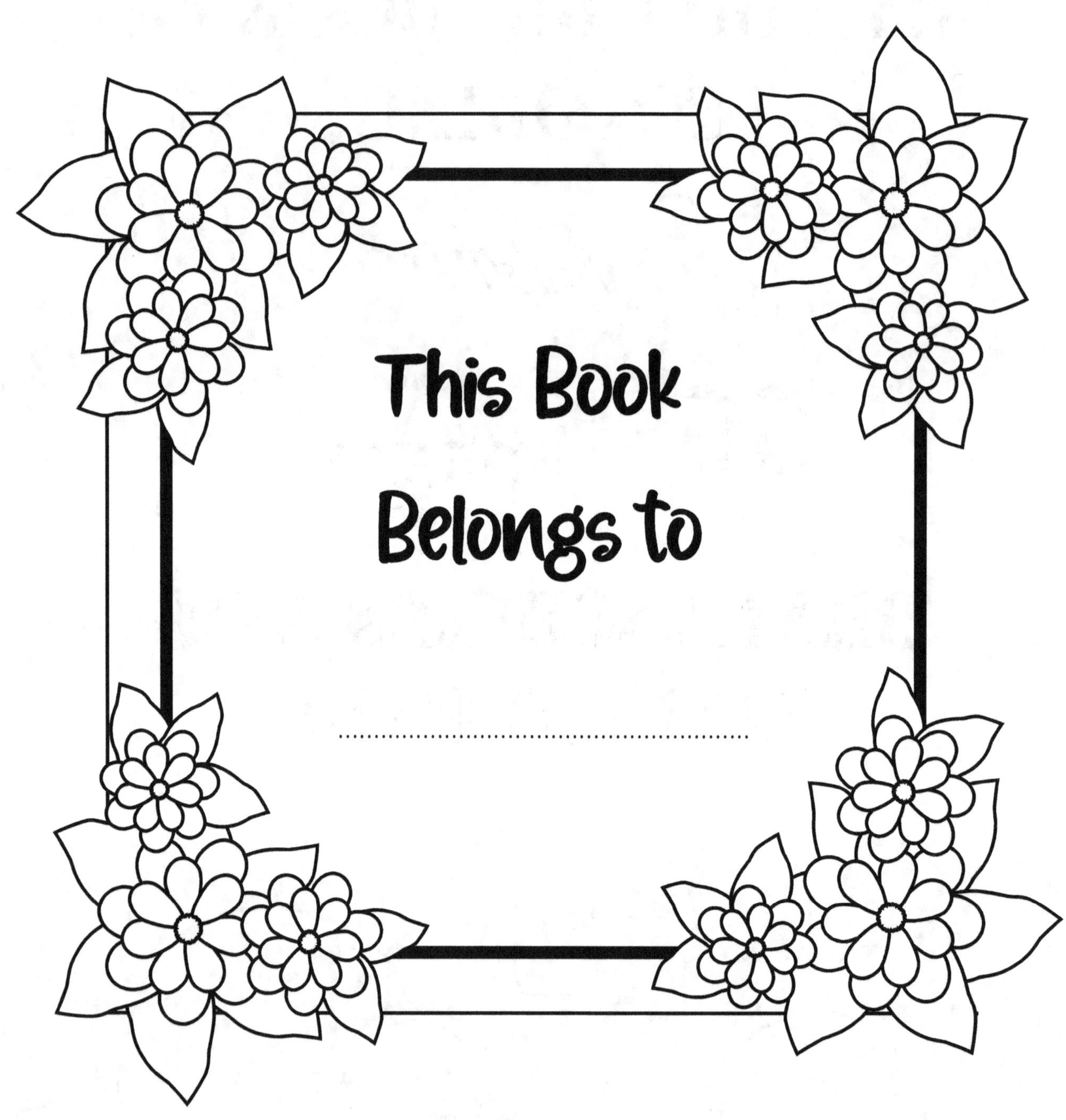
This Book
Belongs to
....

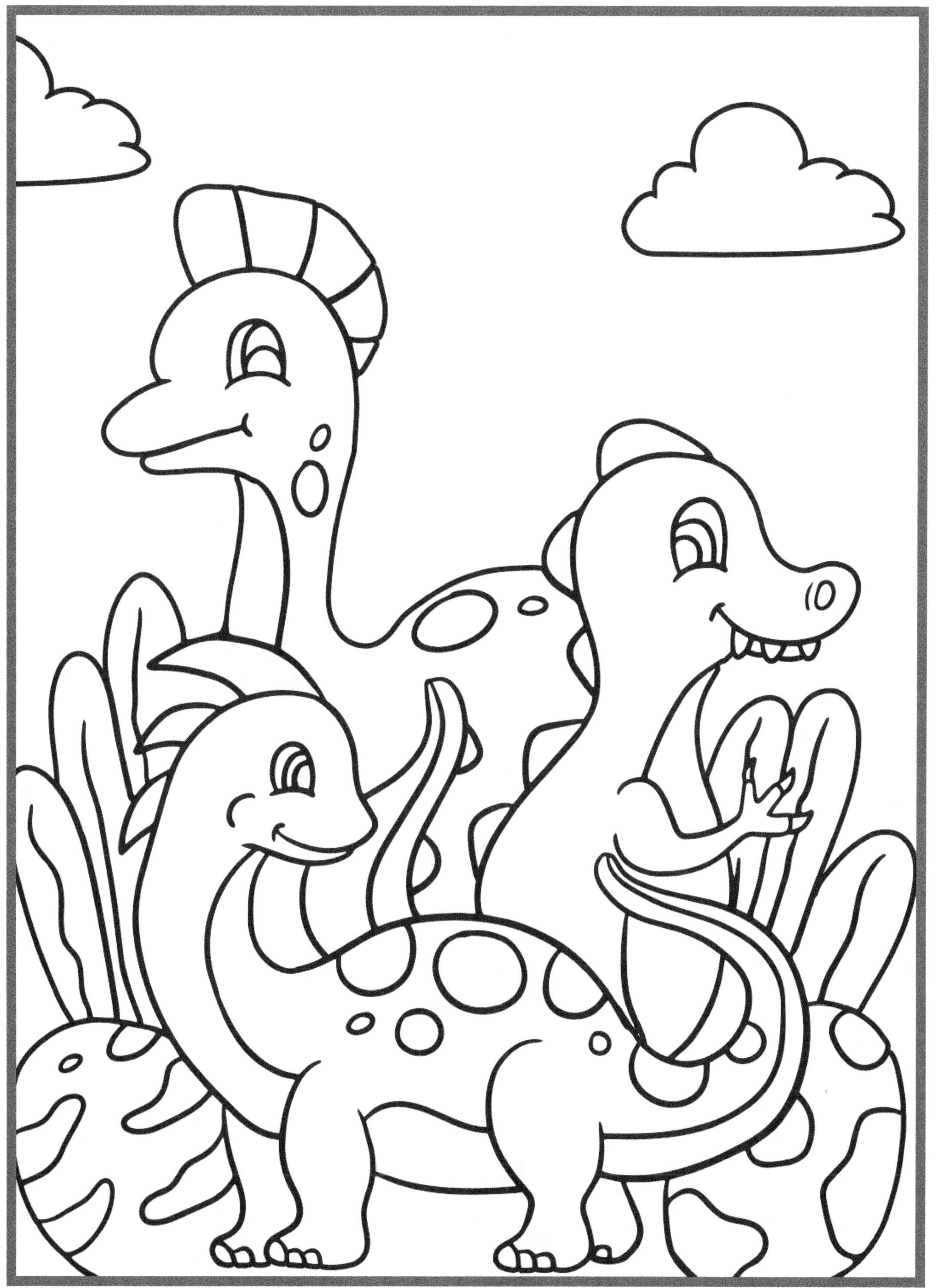

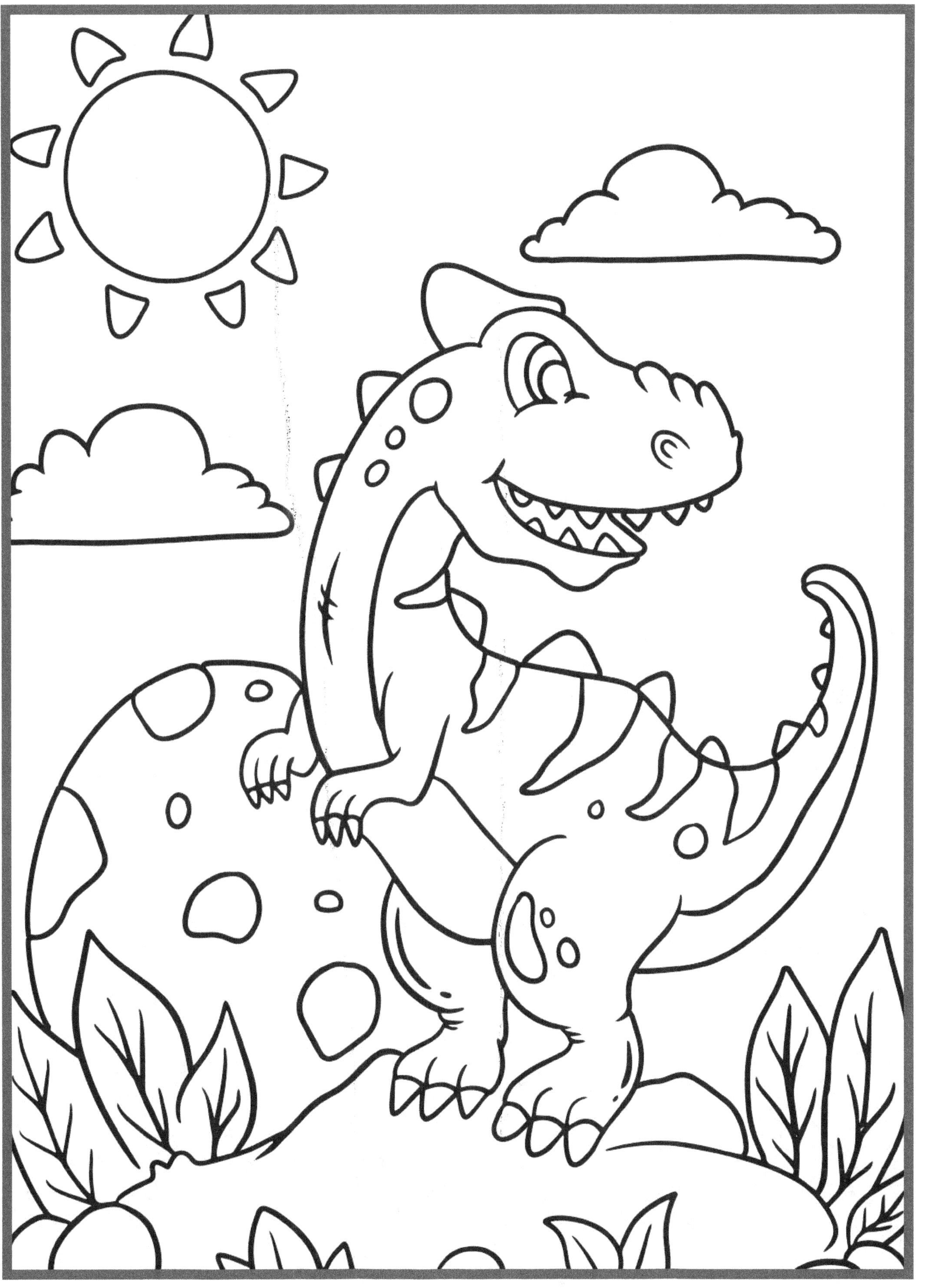

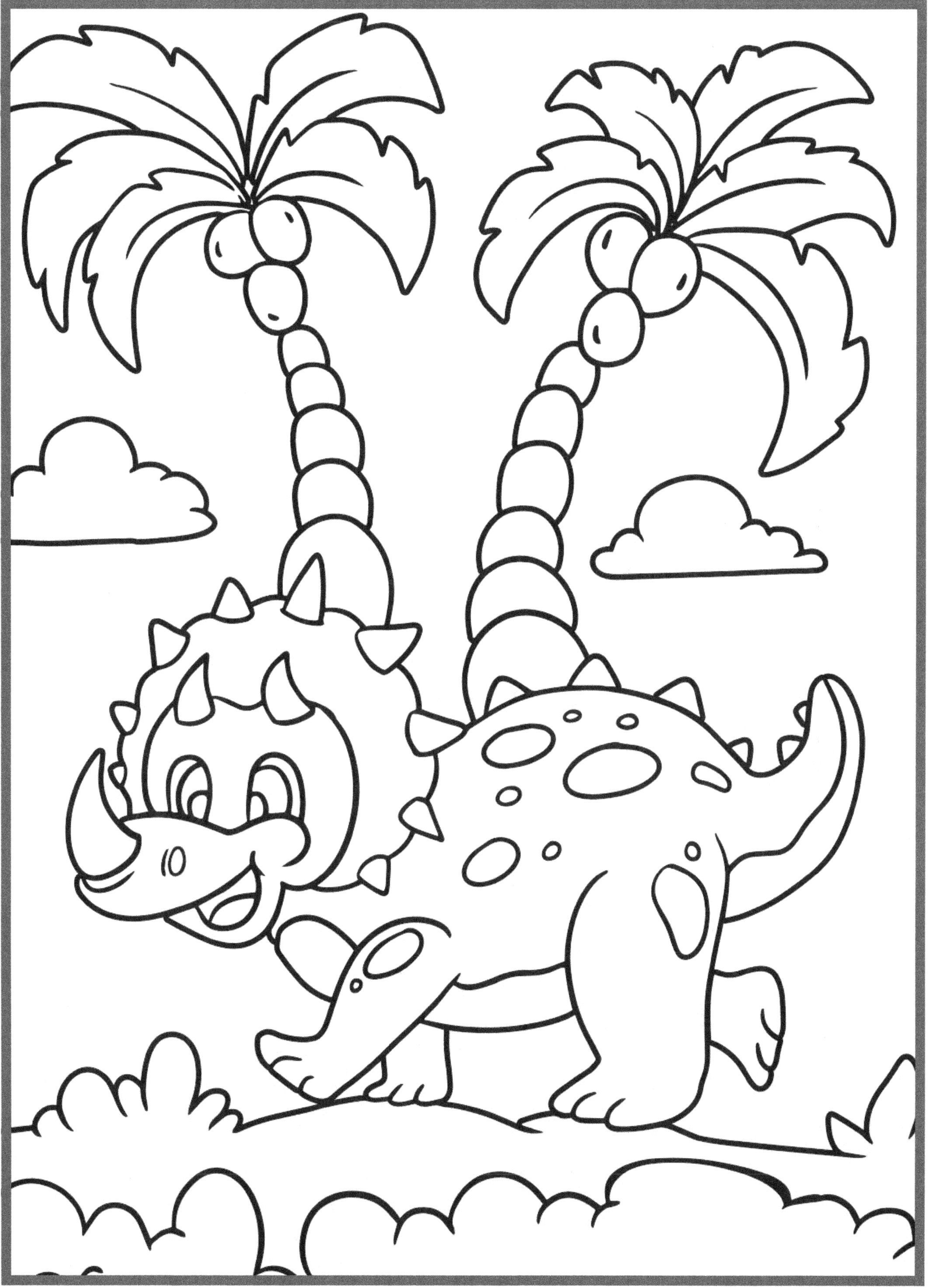

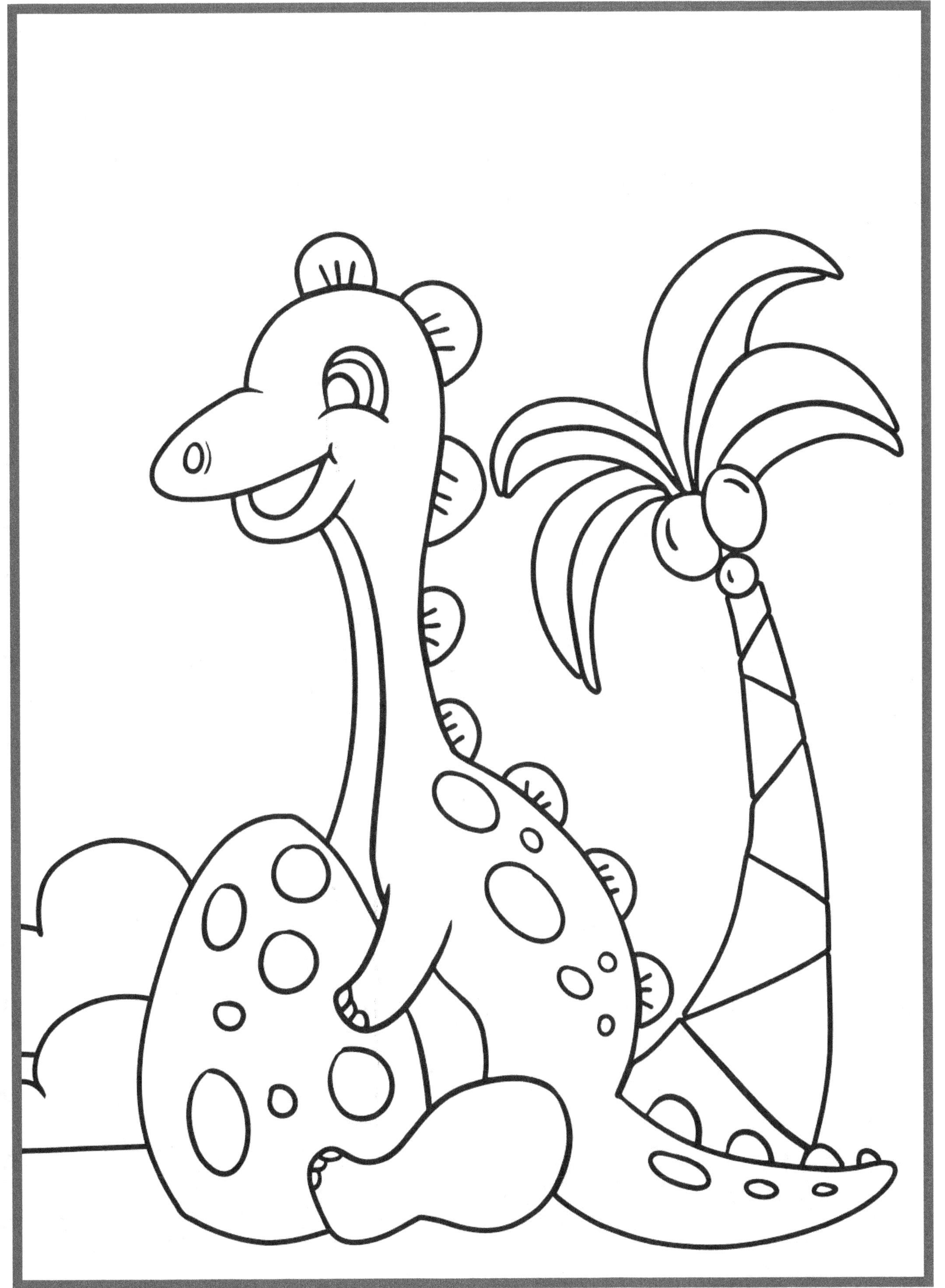

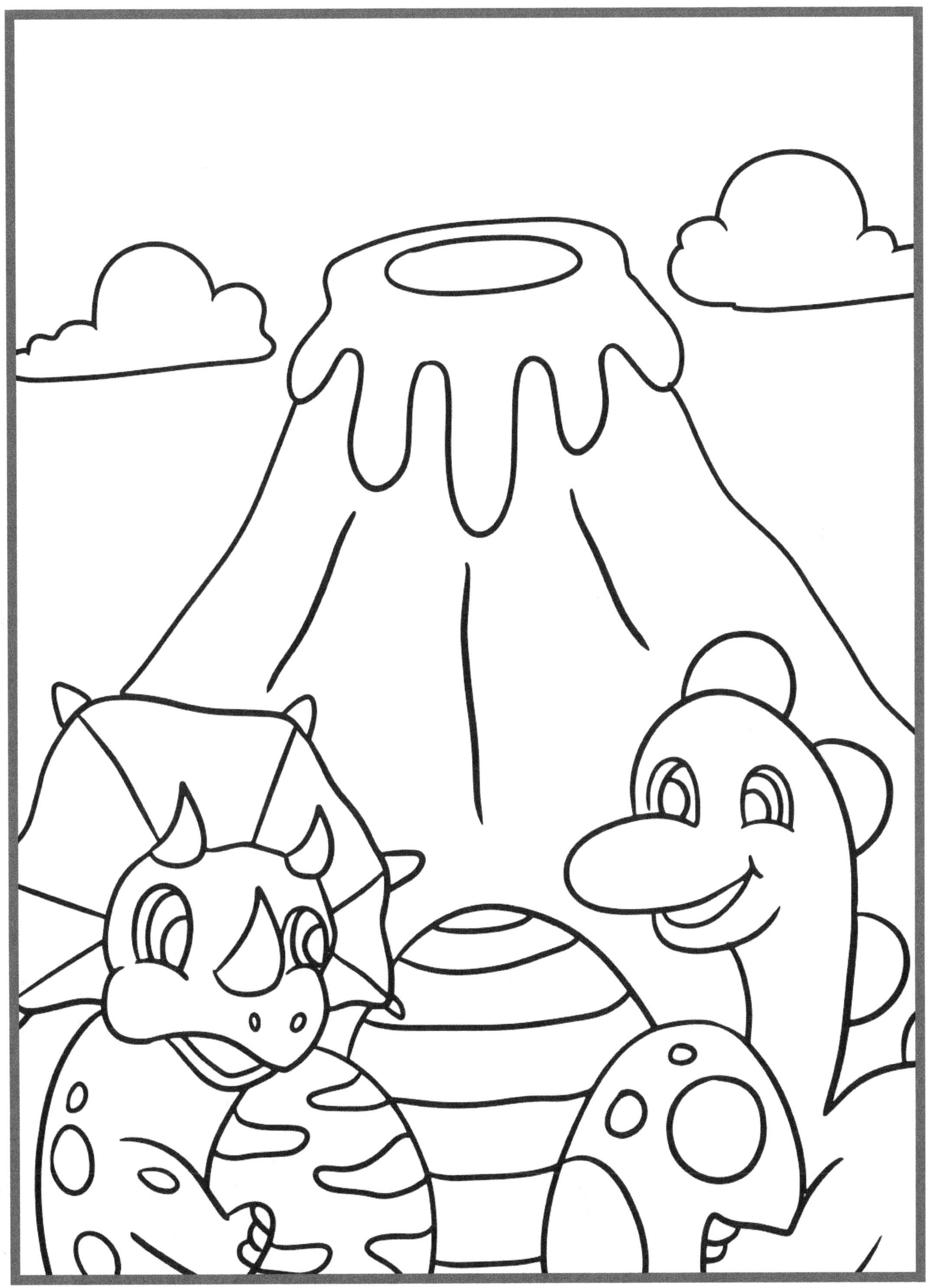

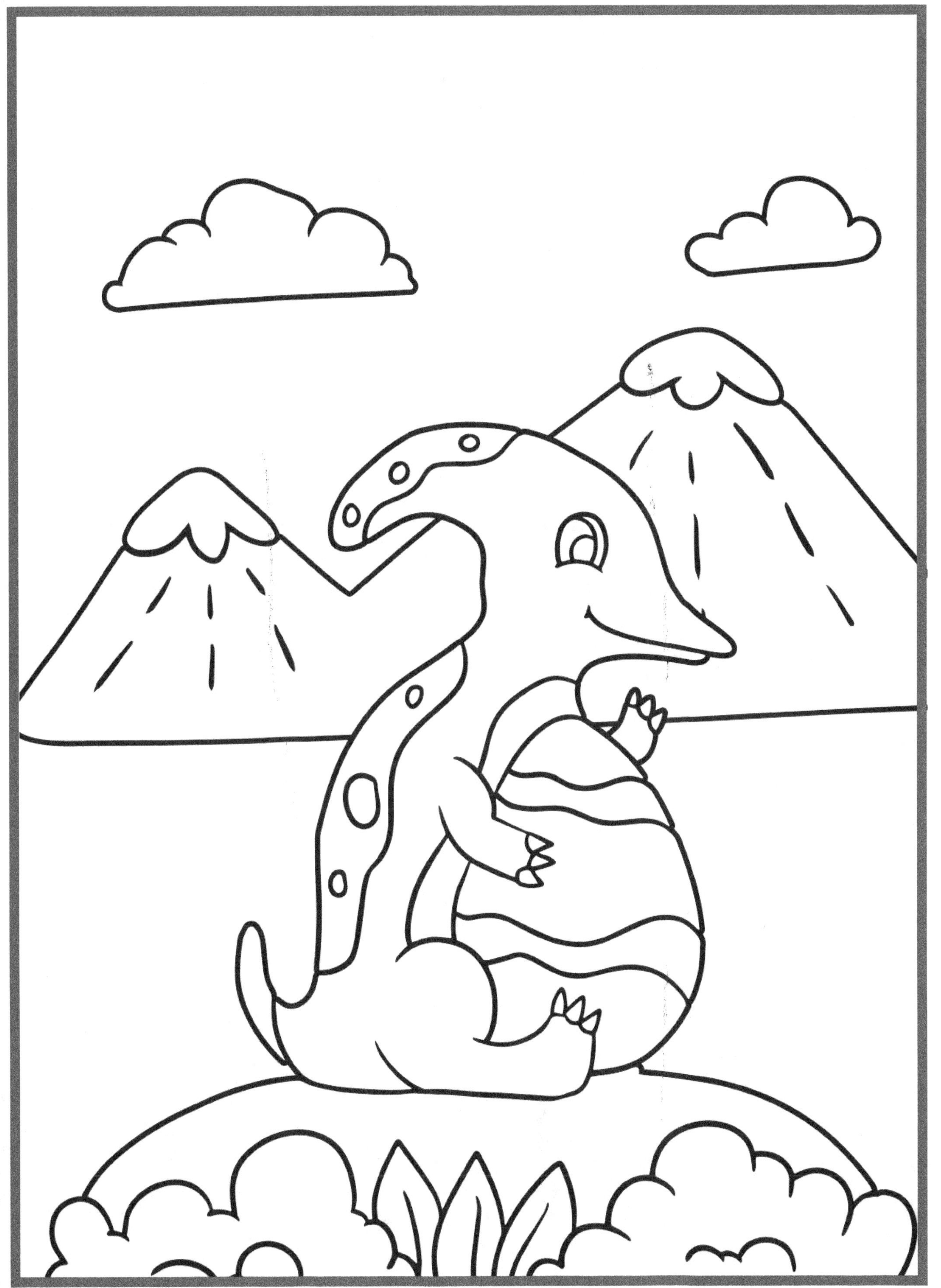

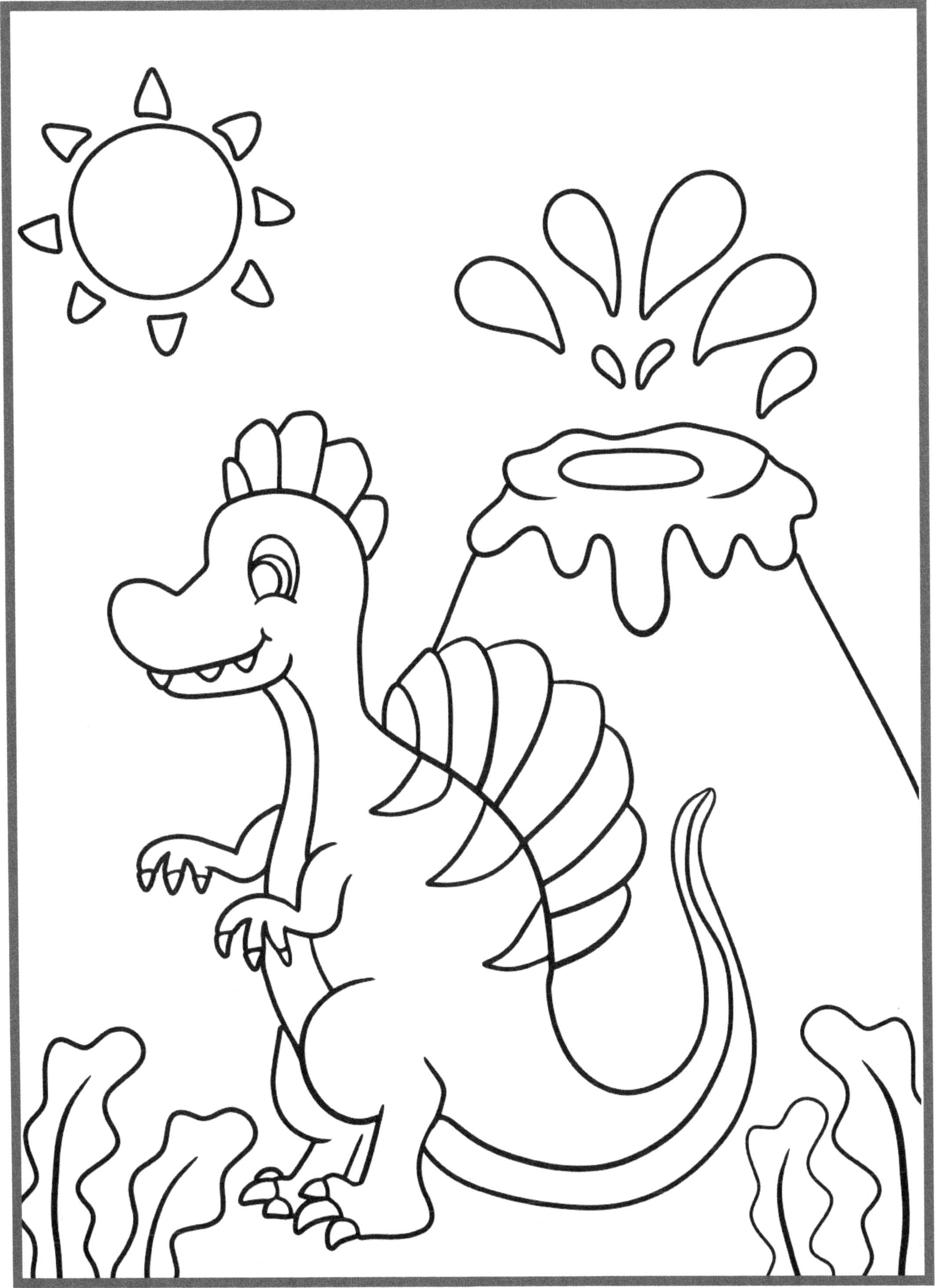

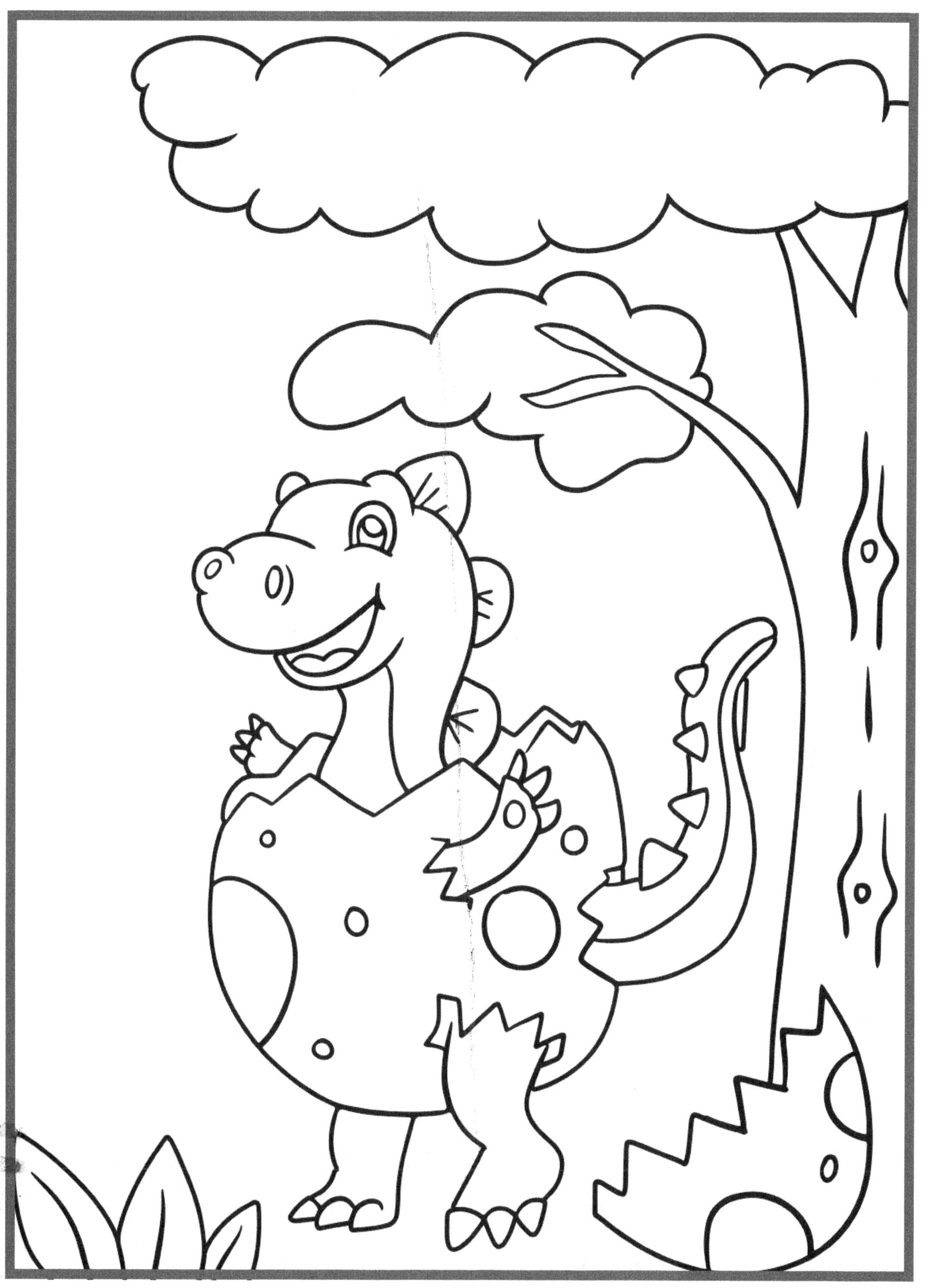

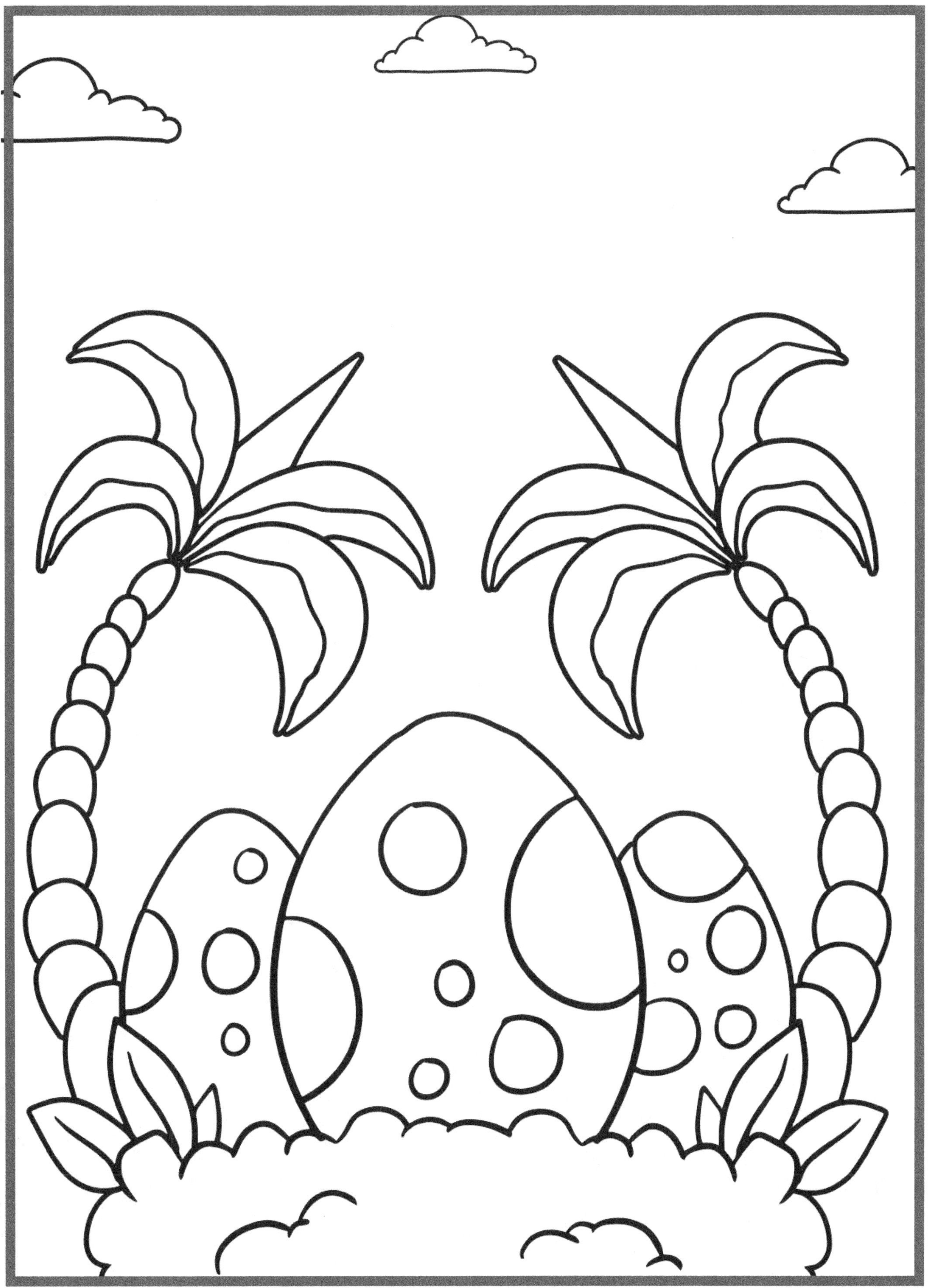

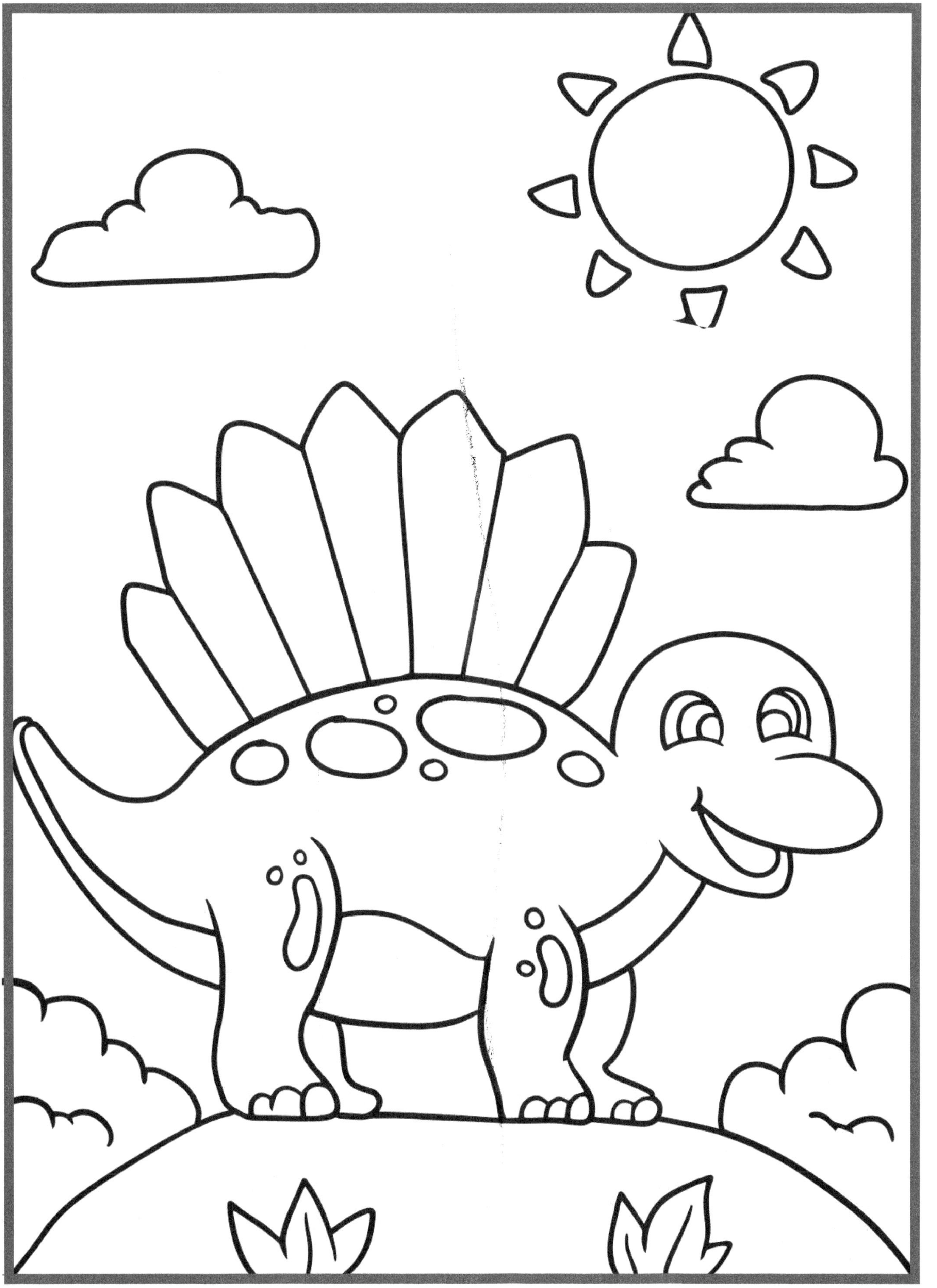

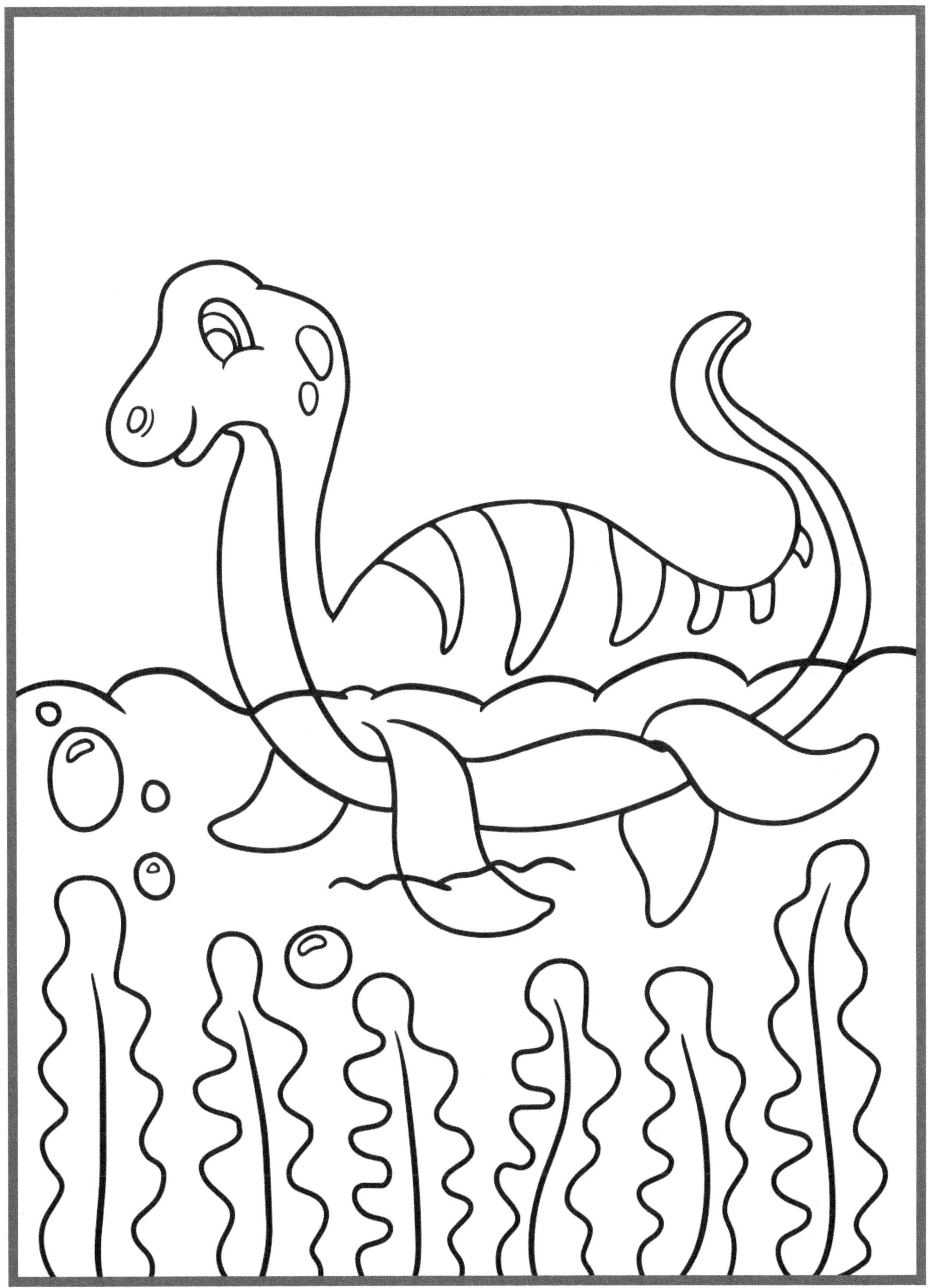

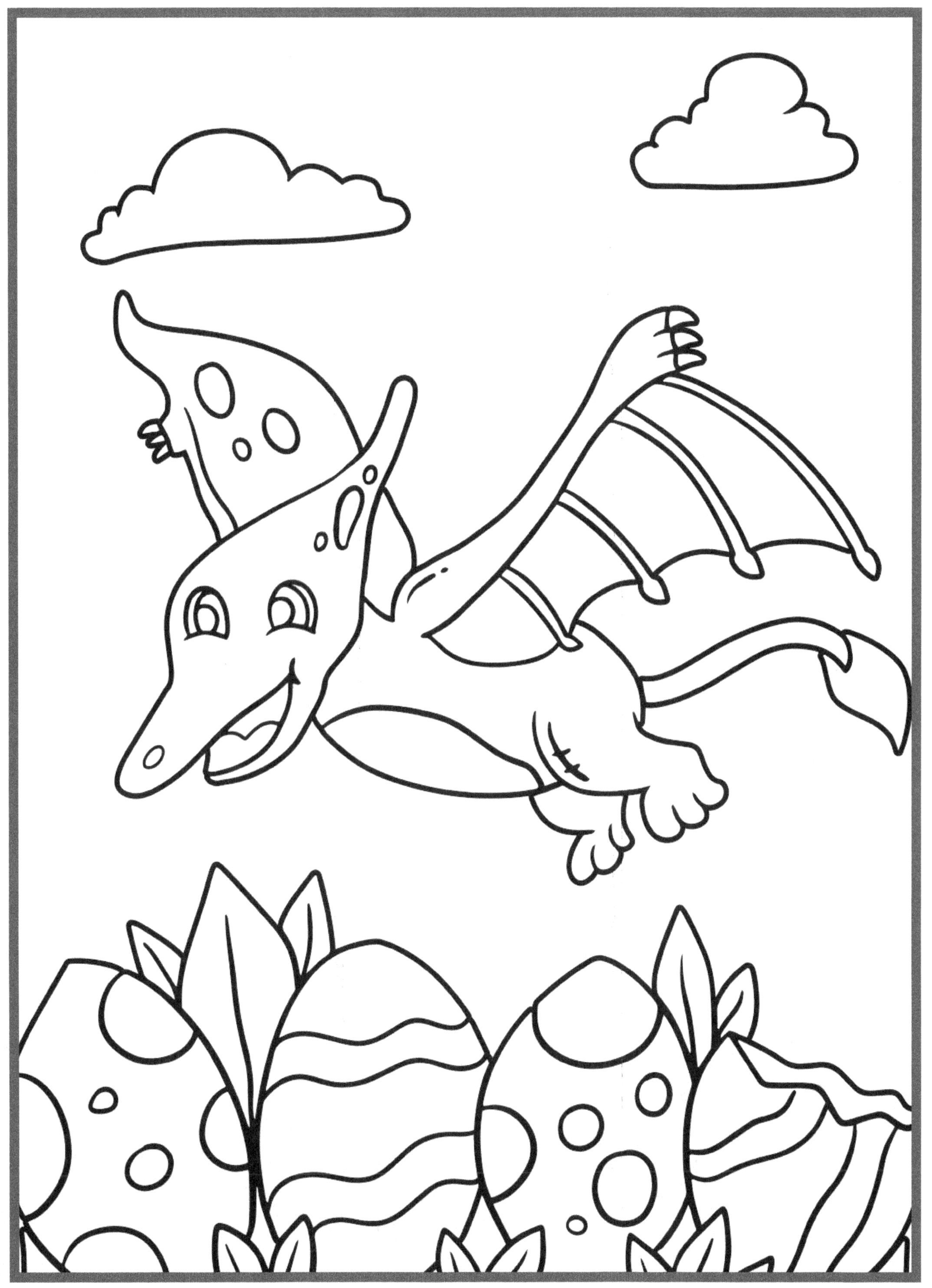

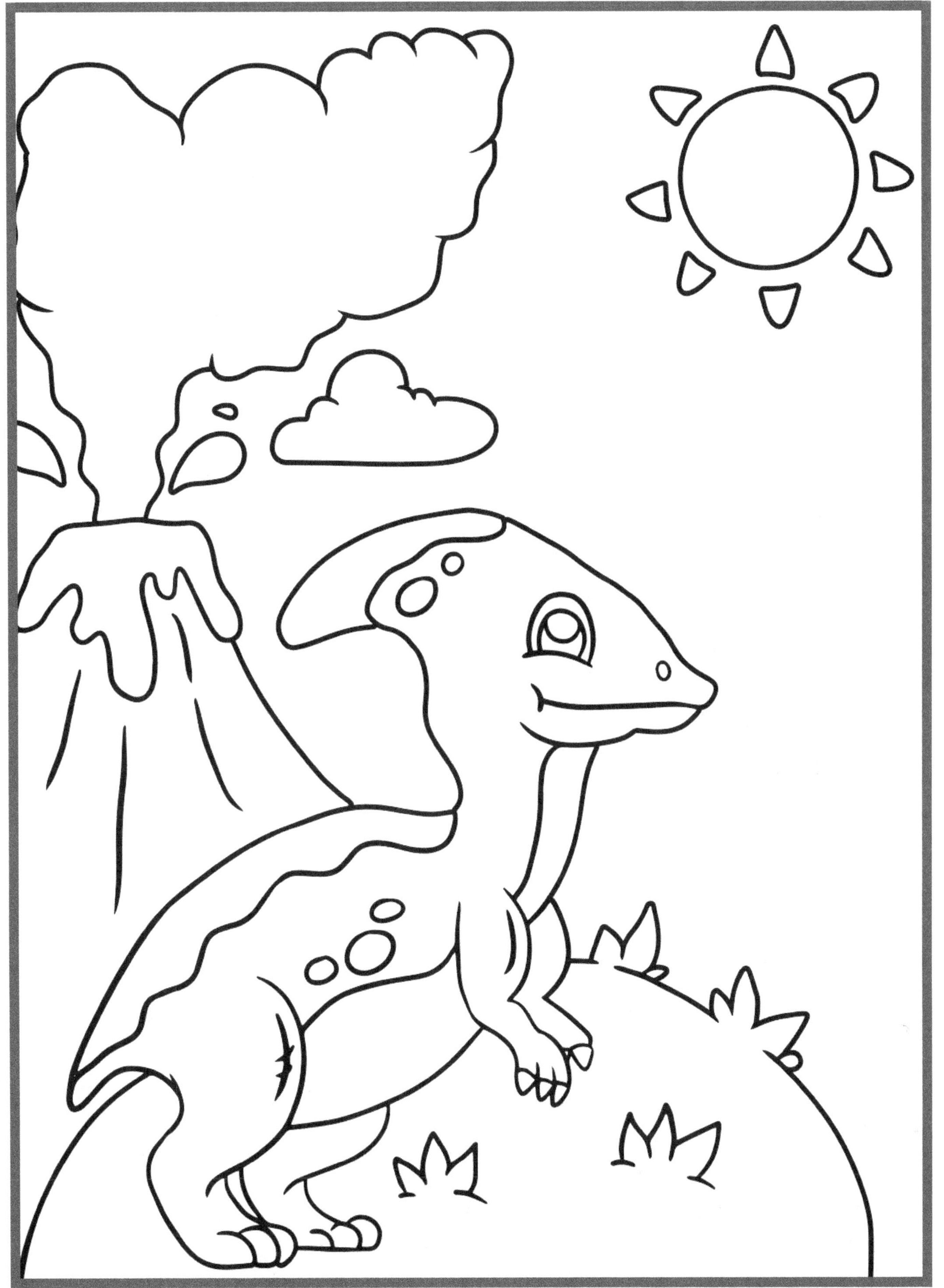

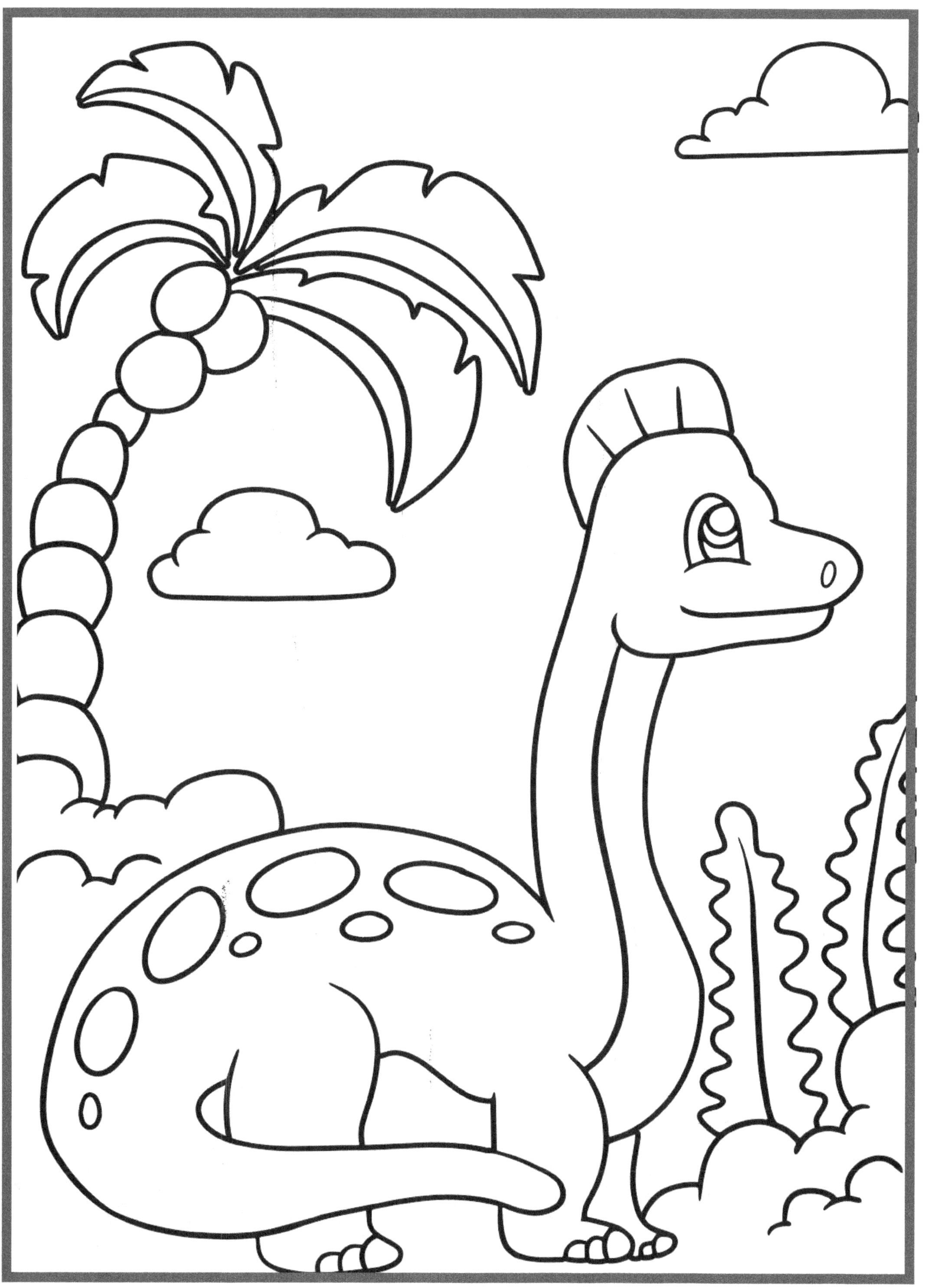

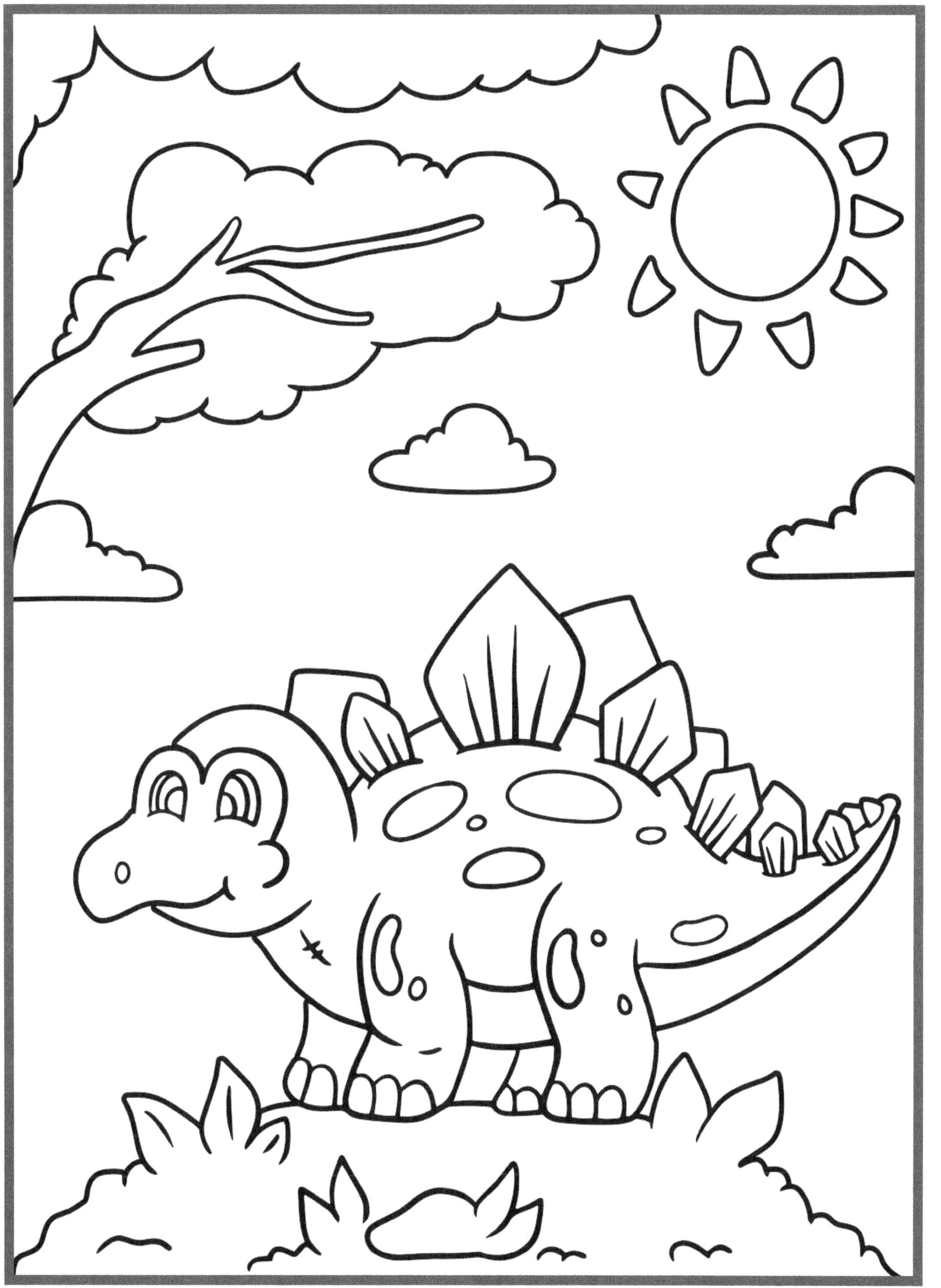

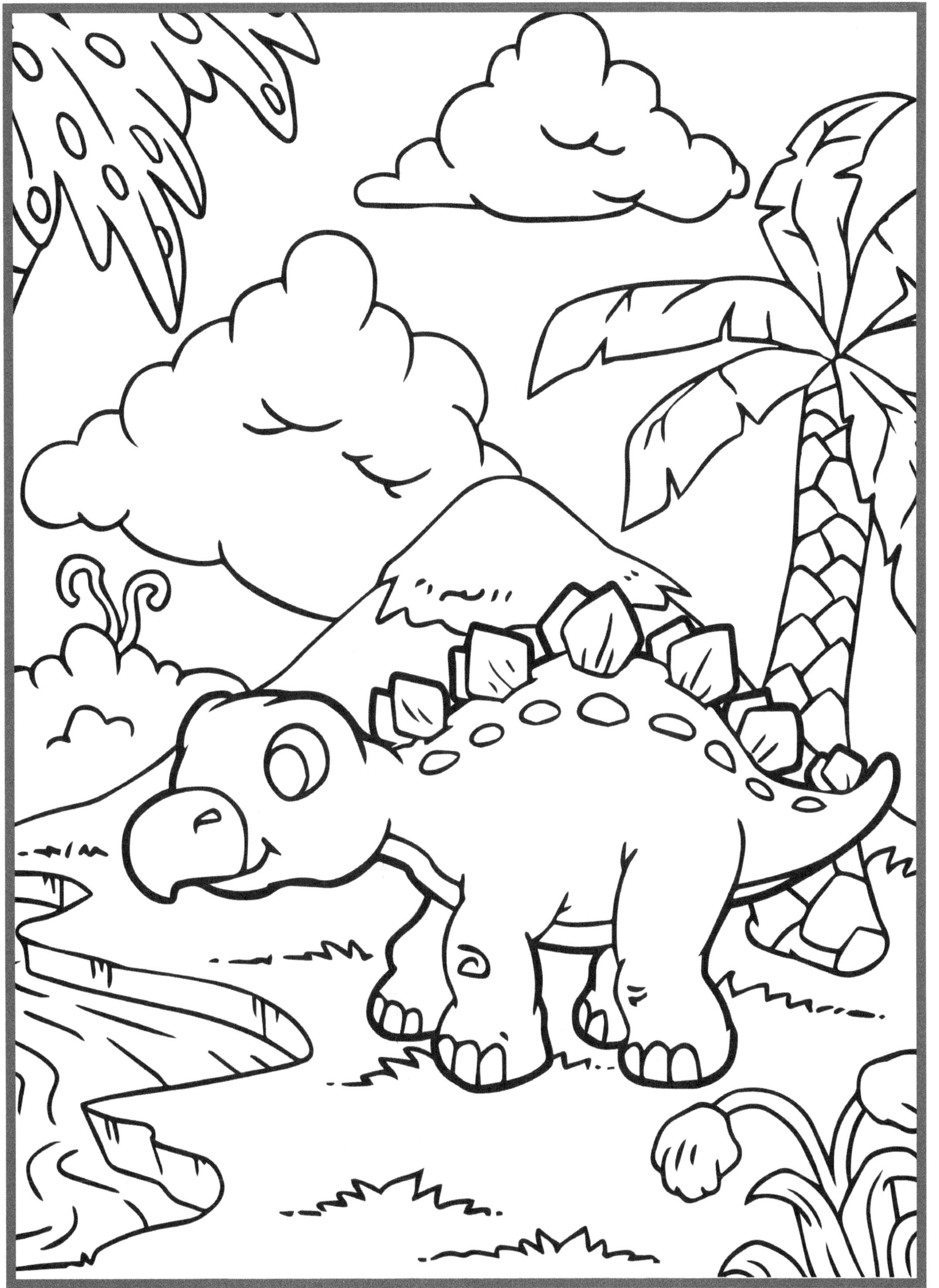

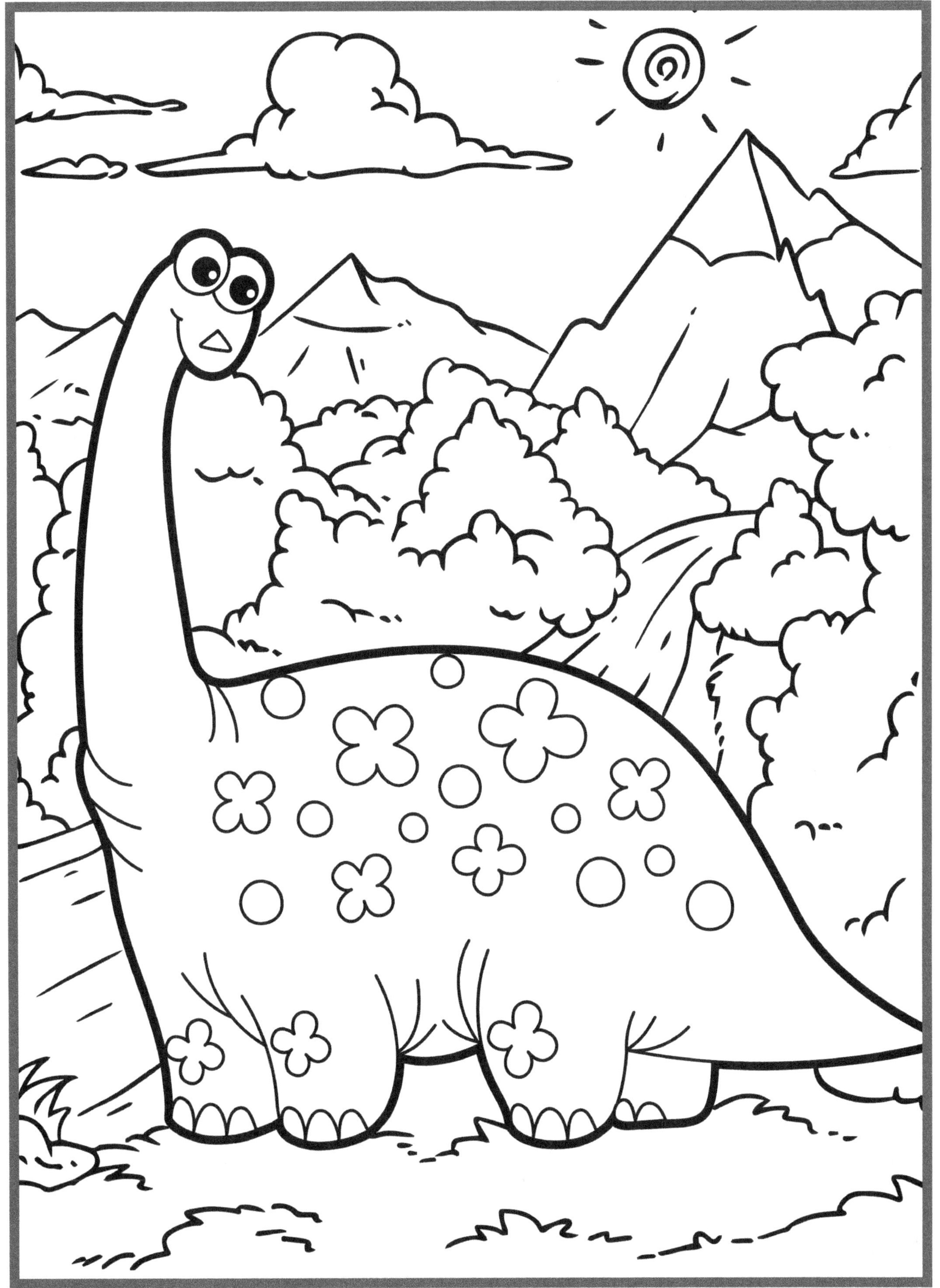

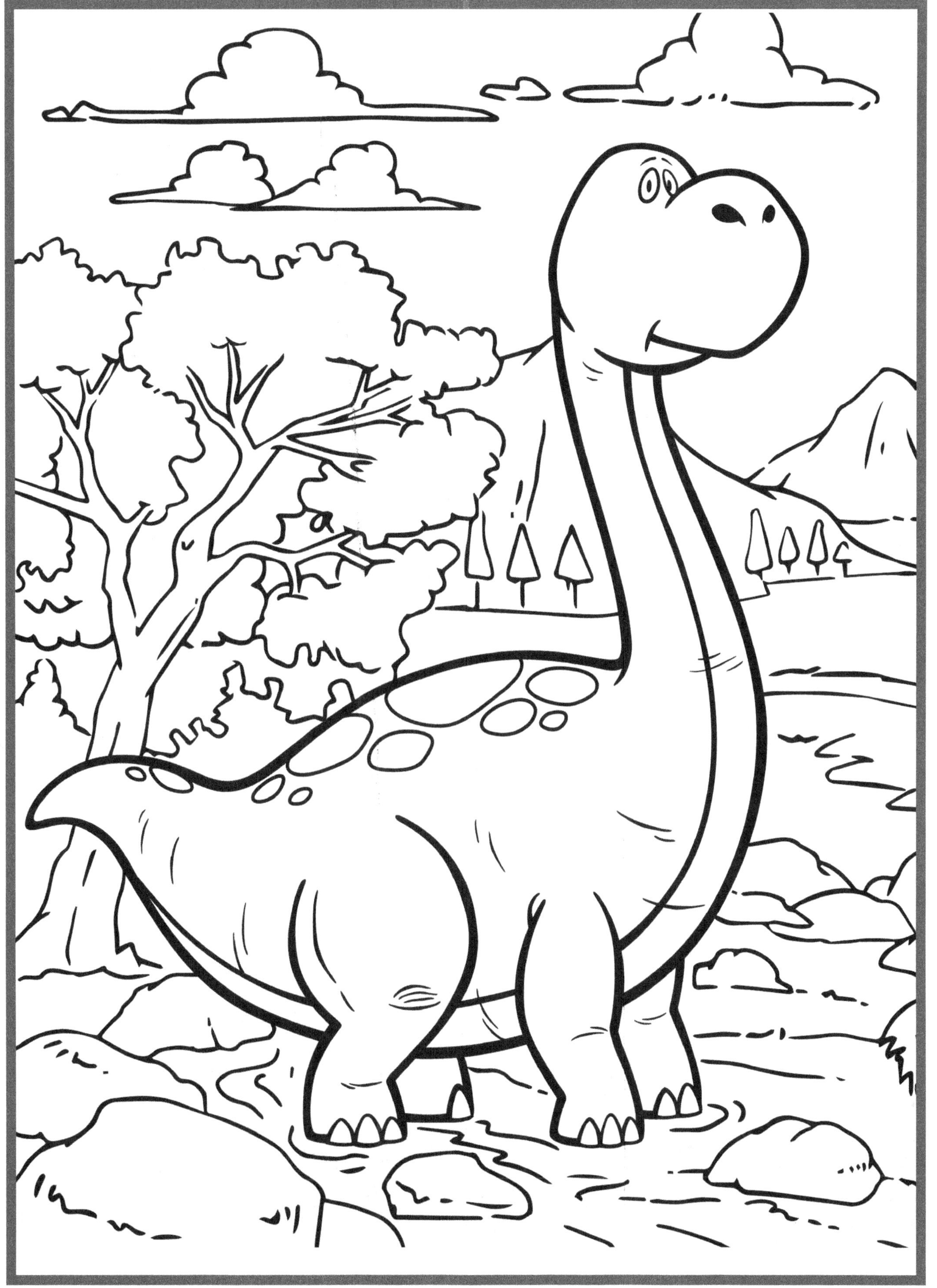

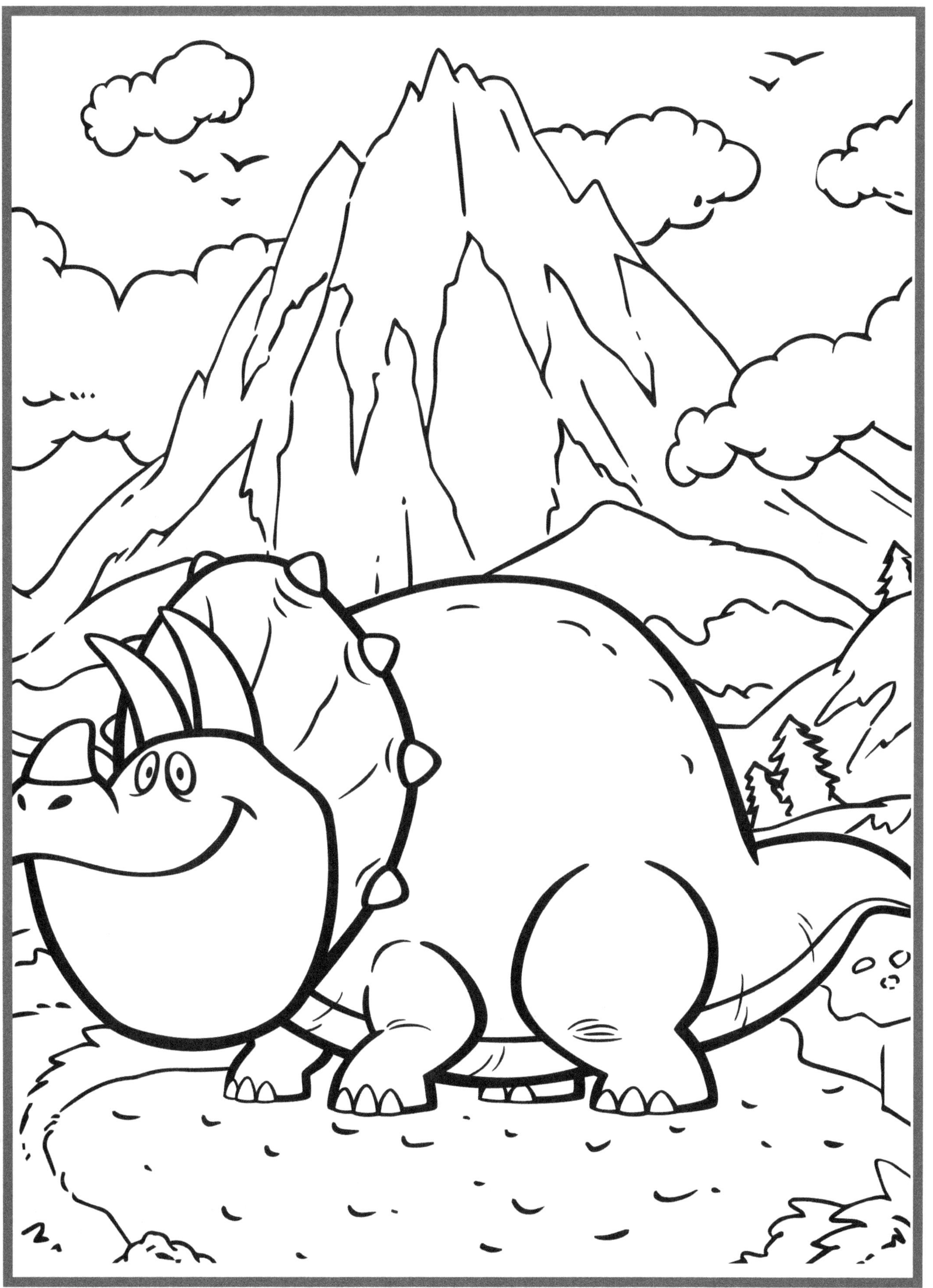

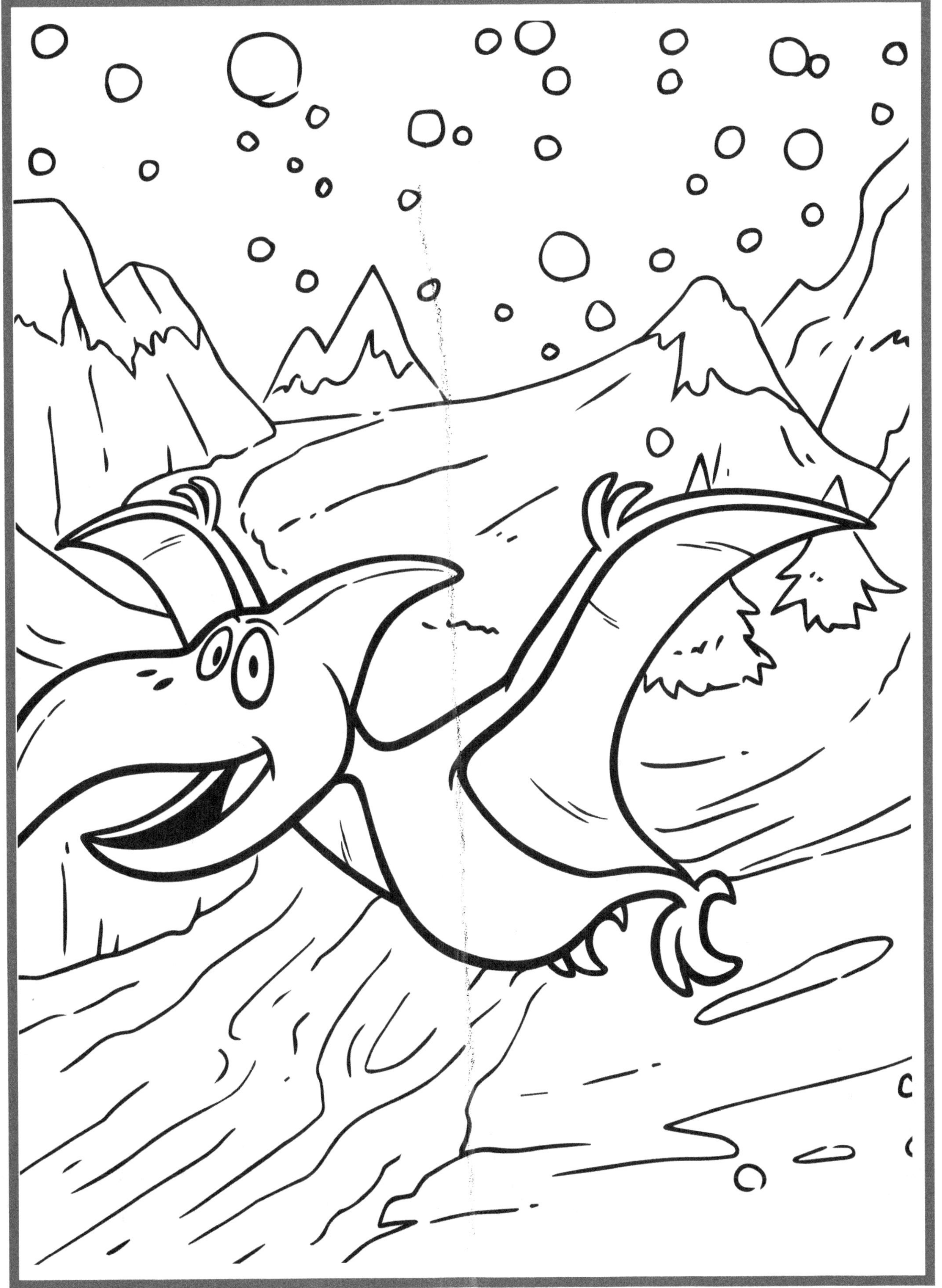

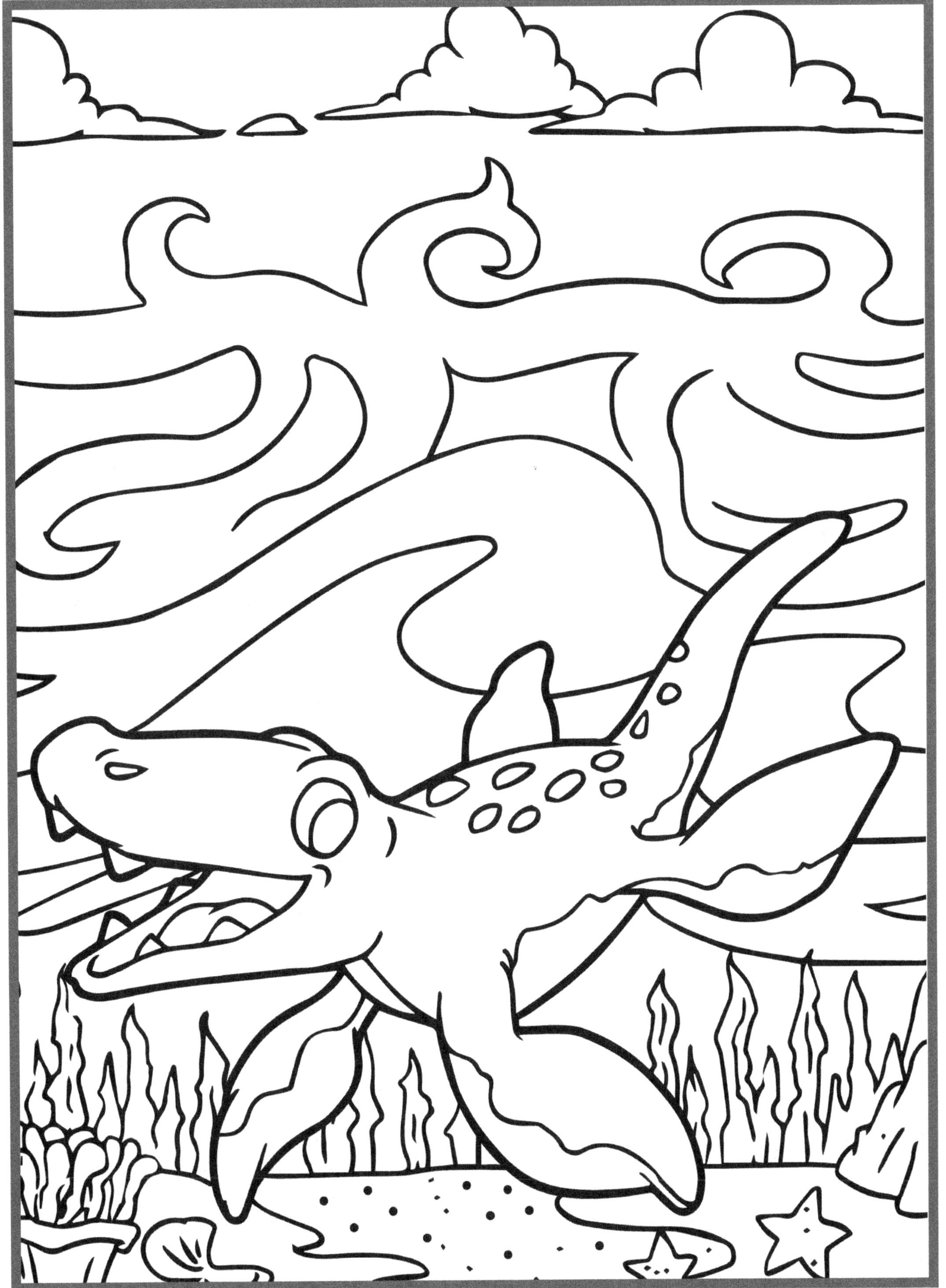

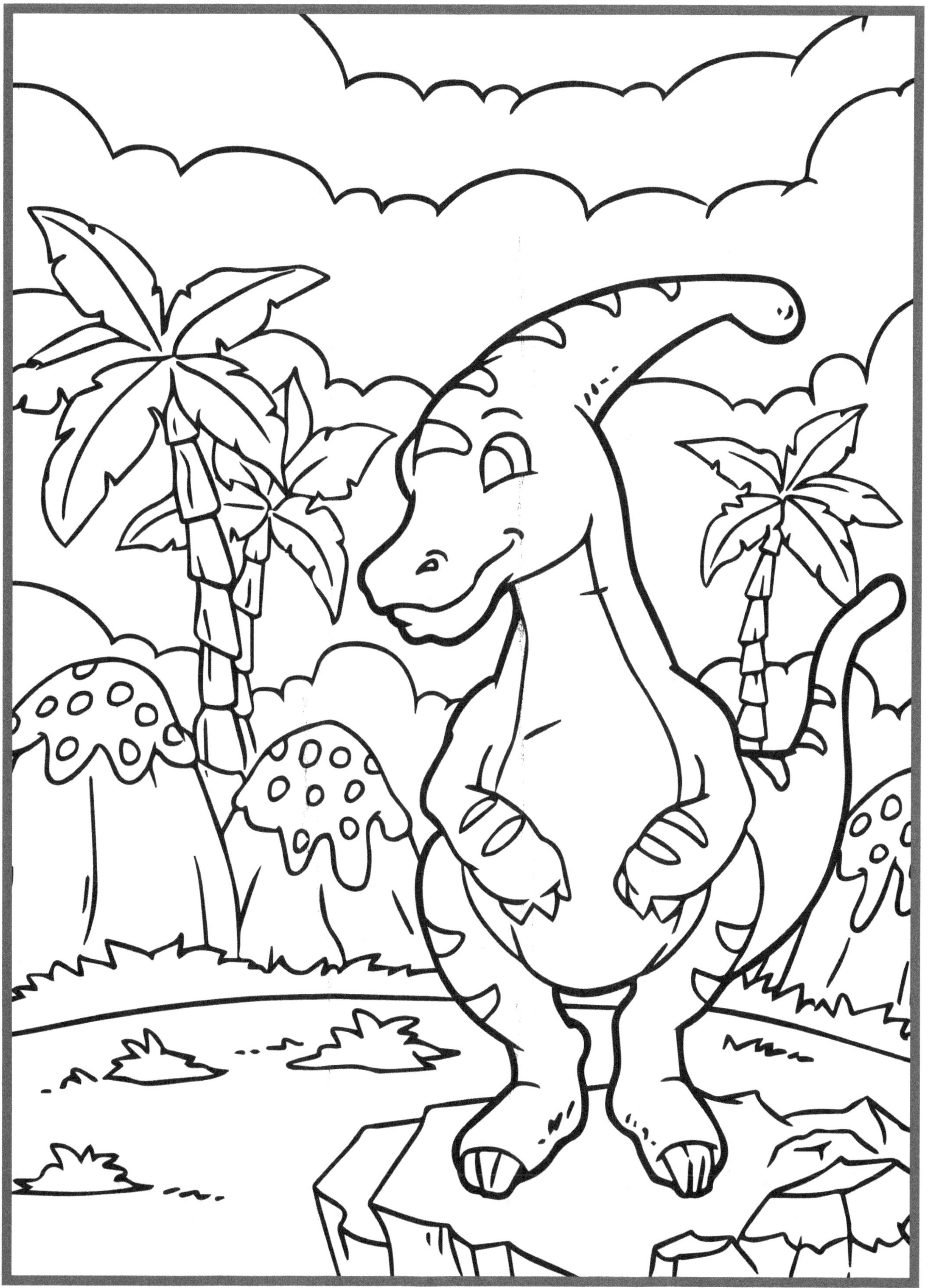

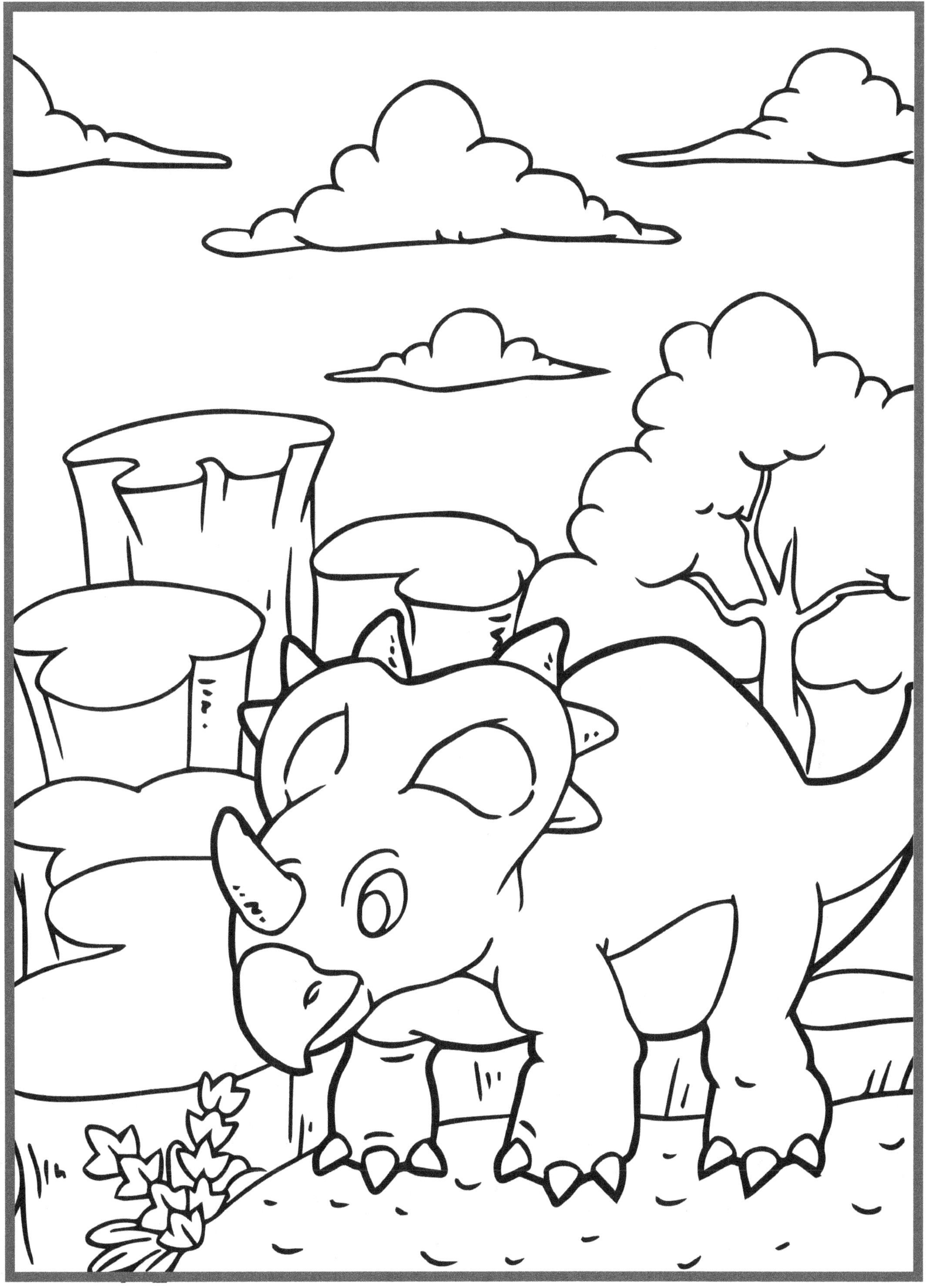

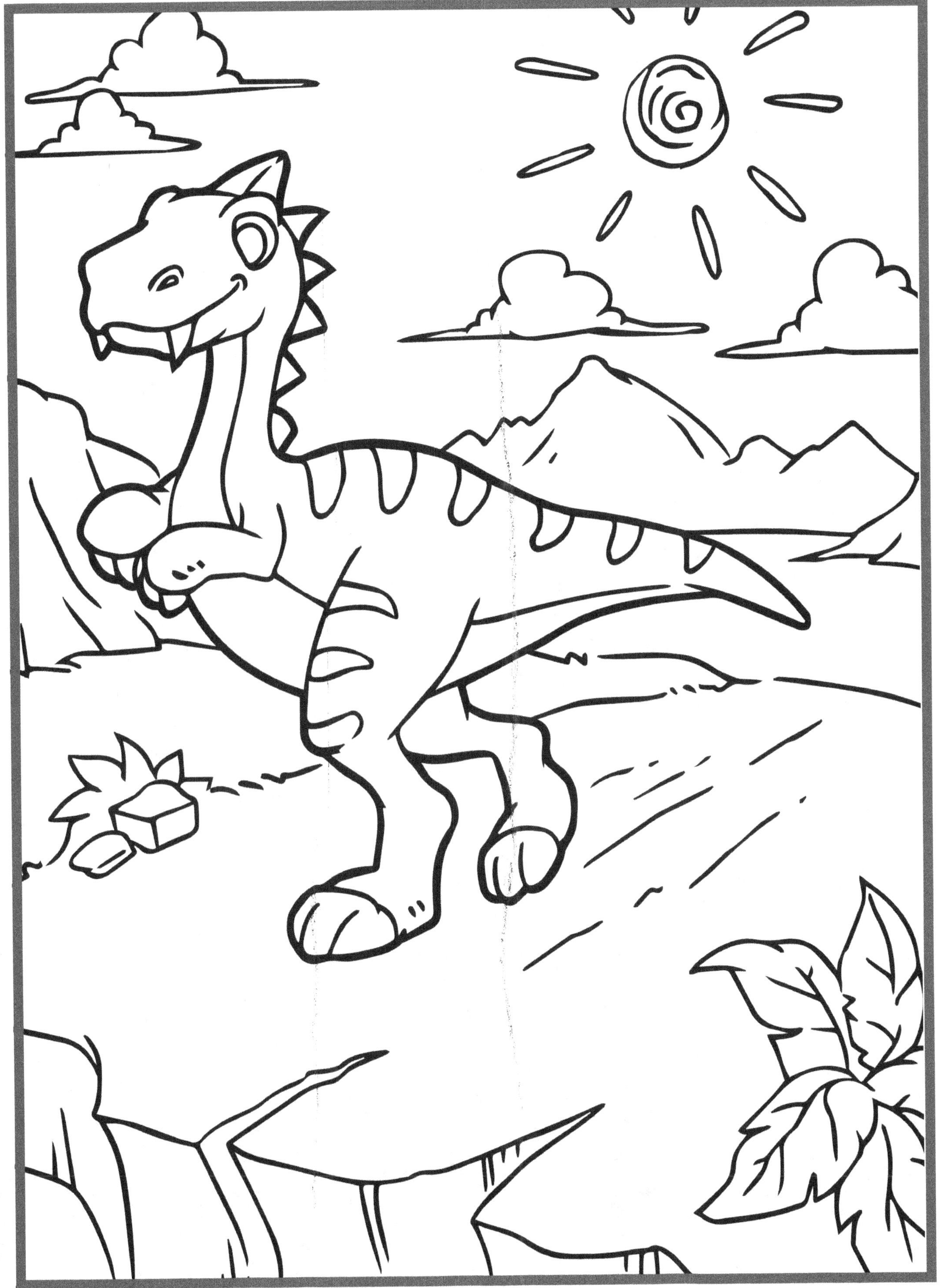

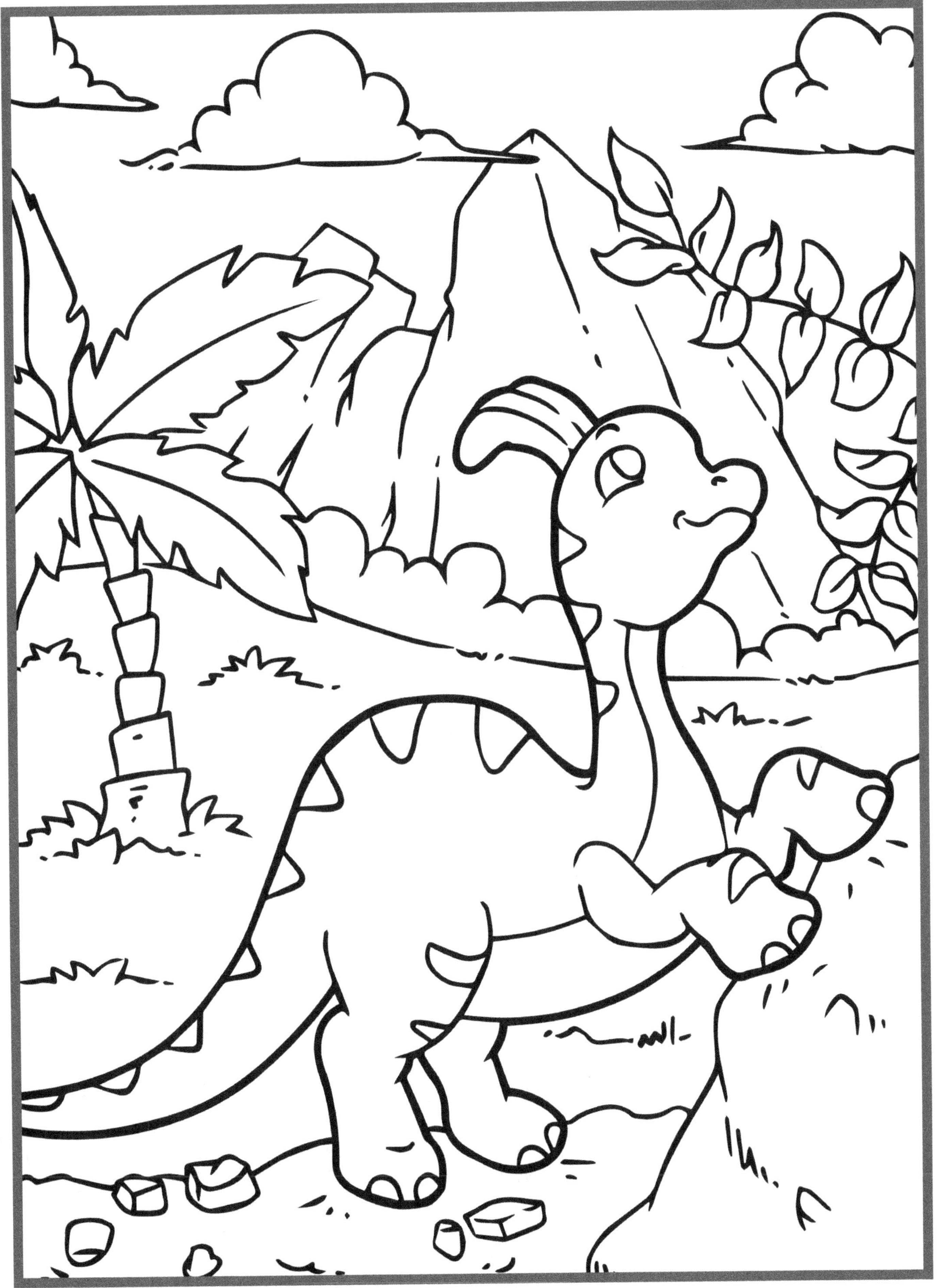

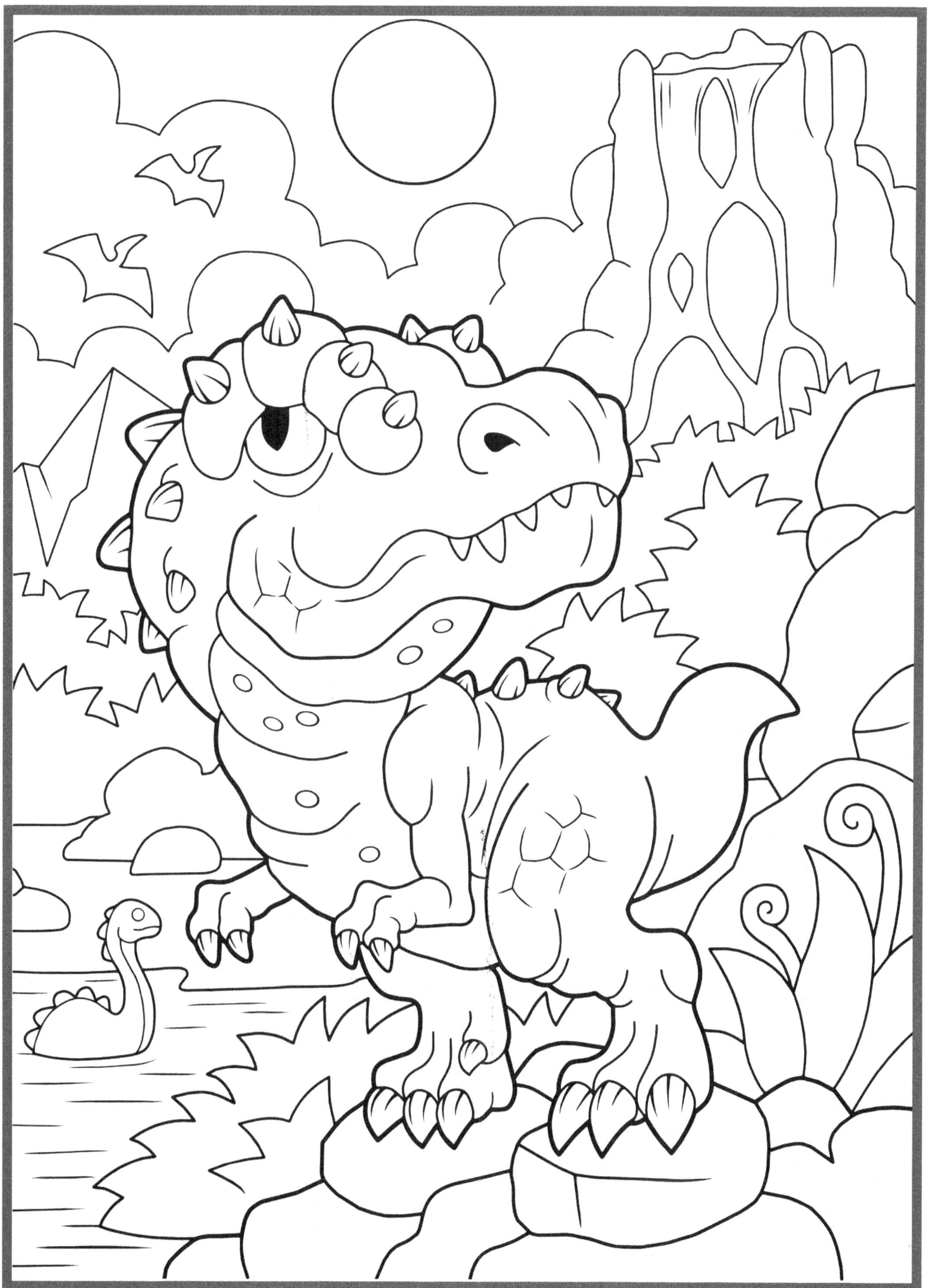

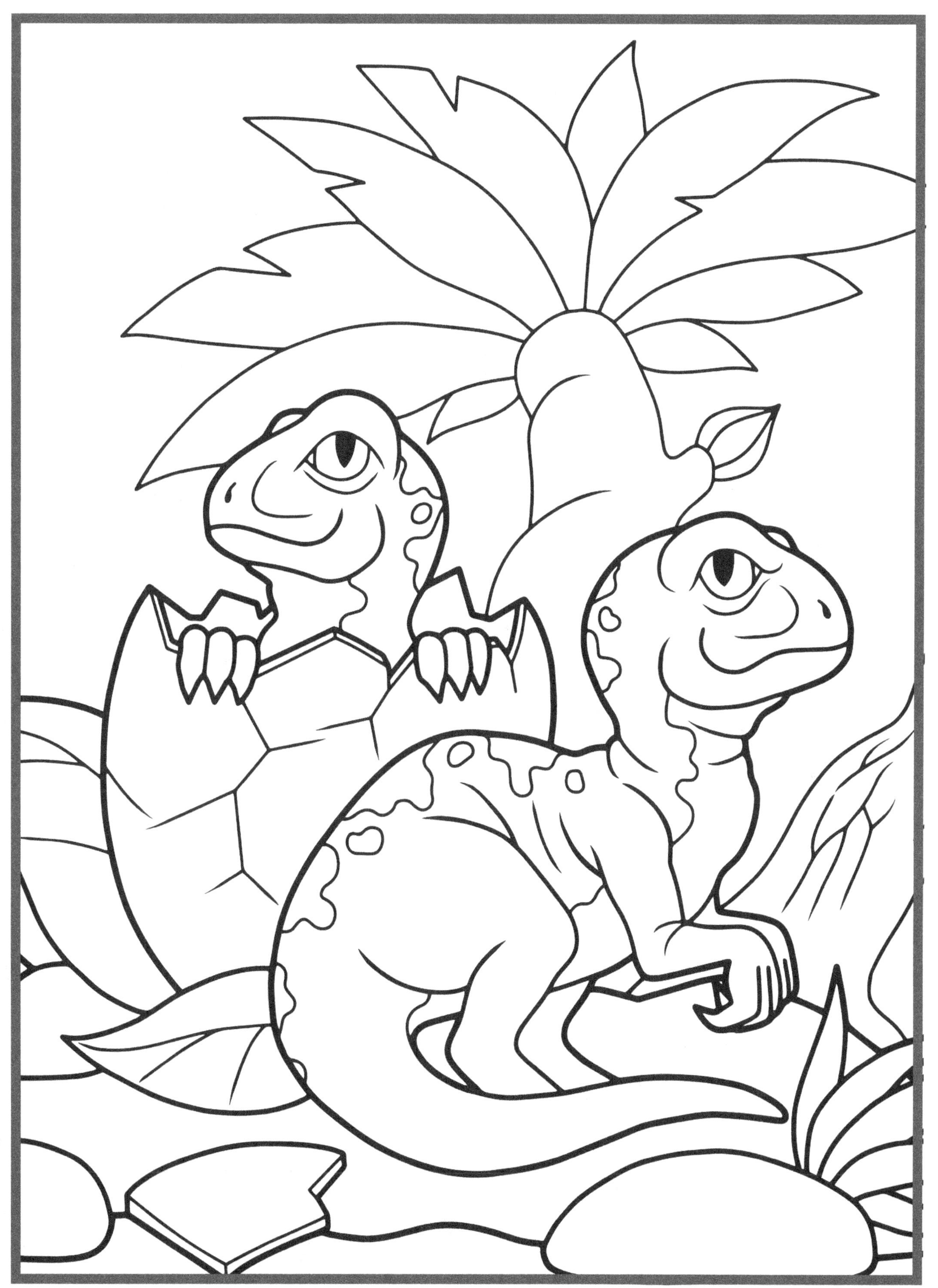

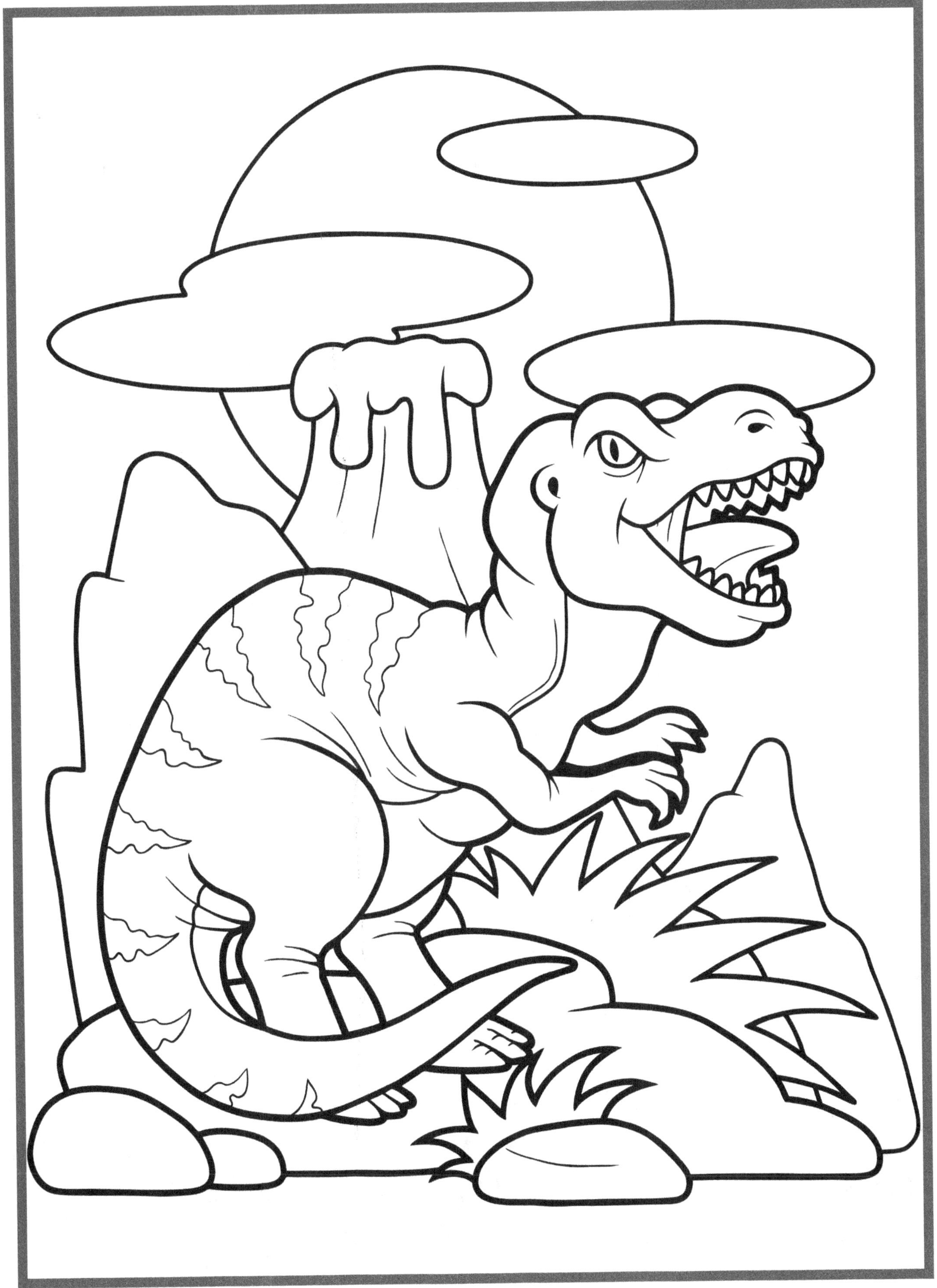

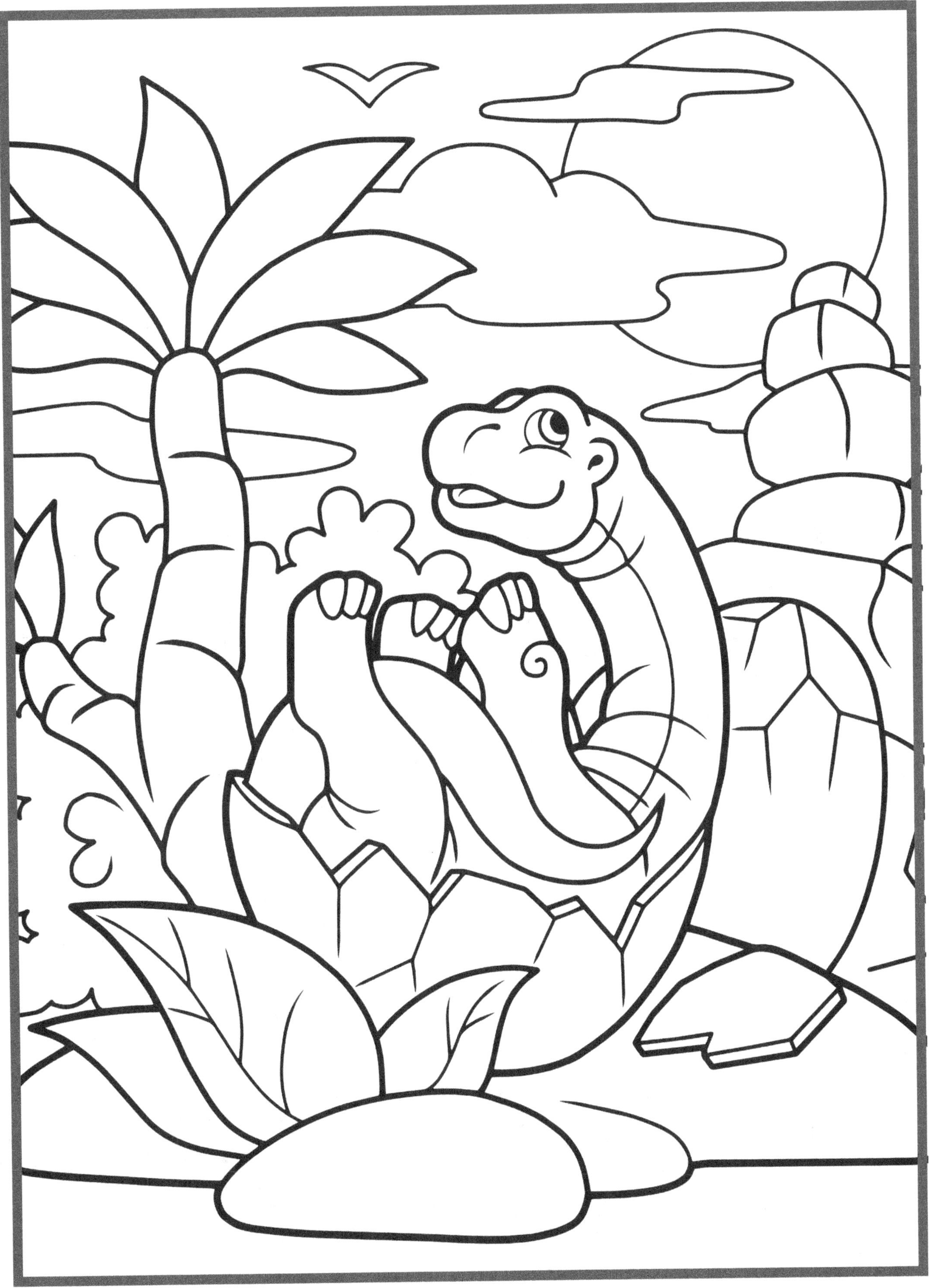

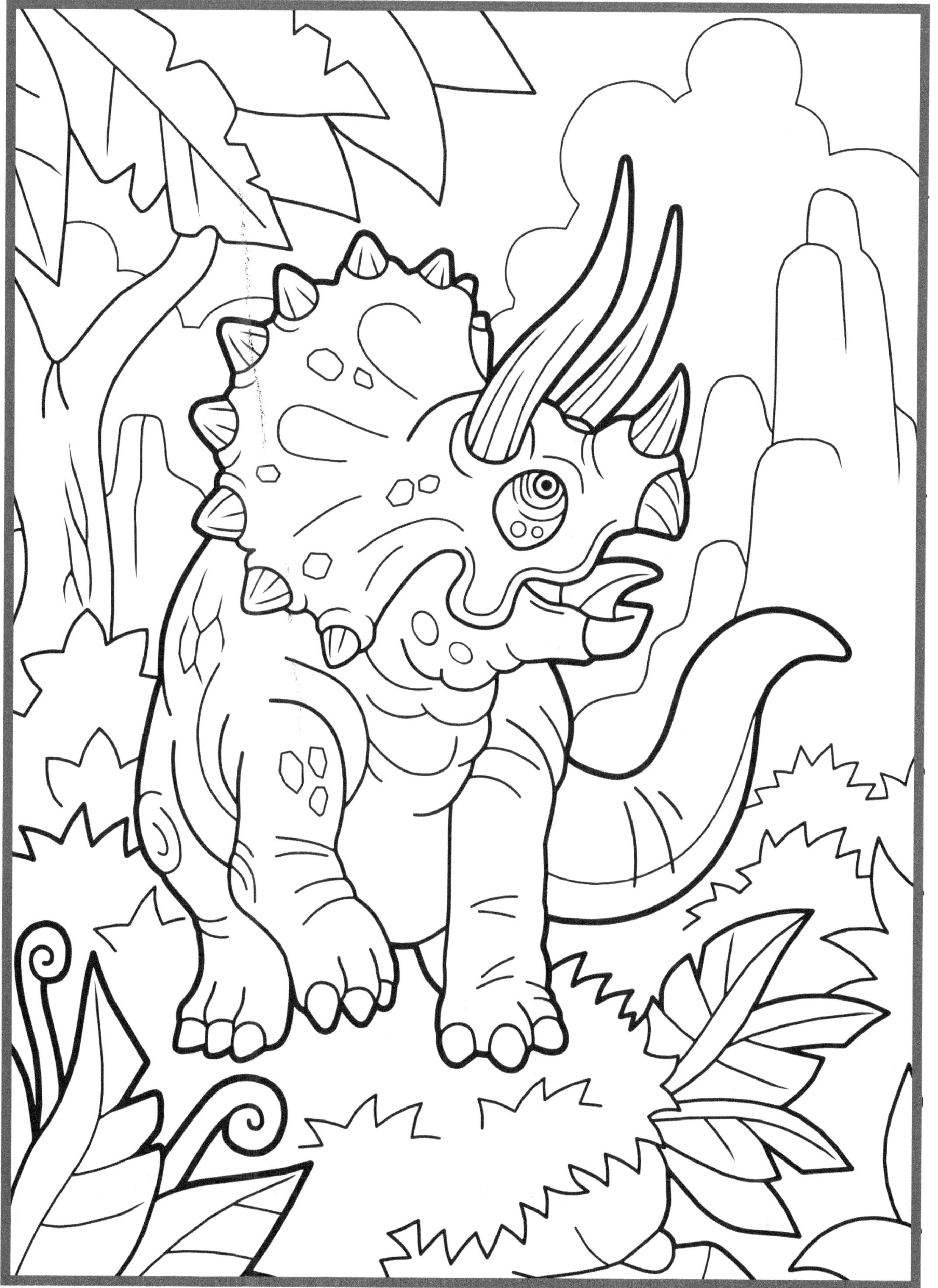

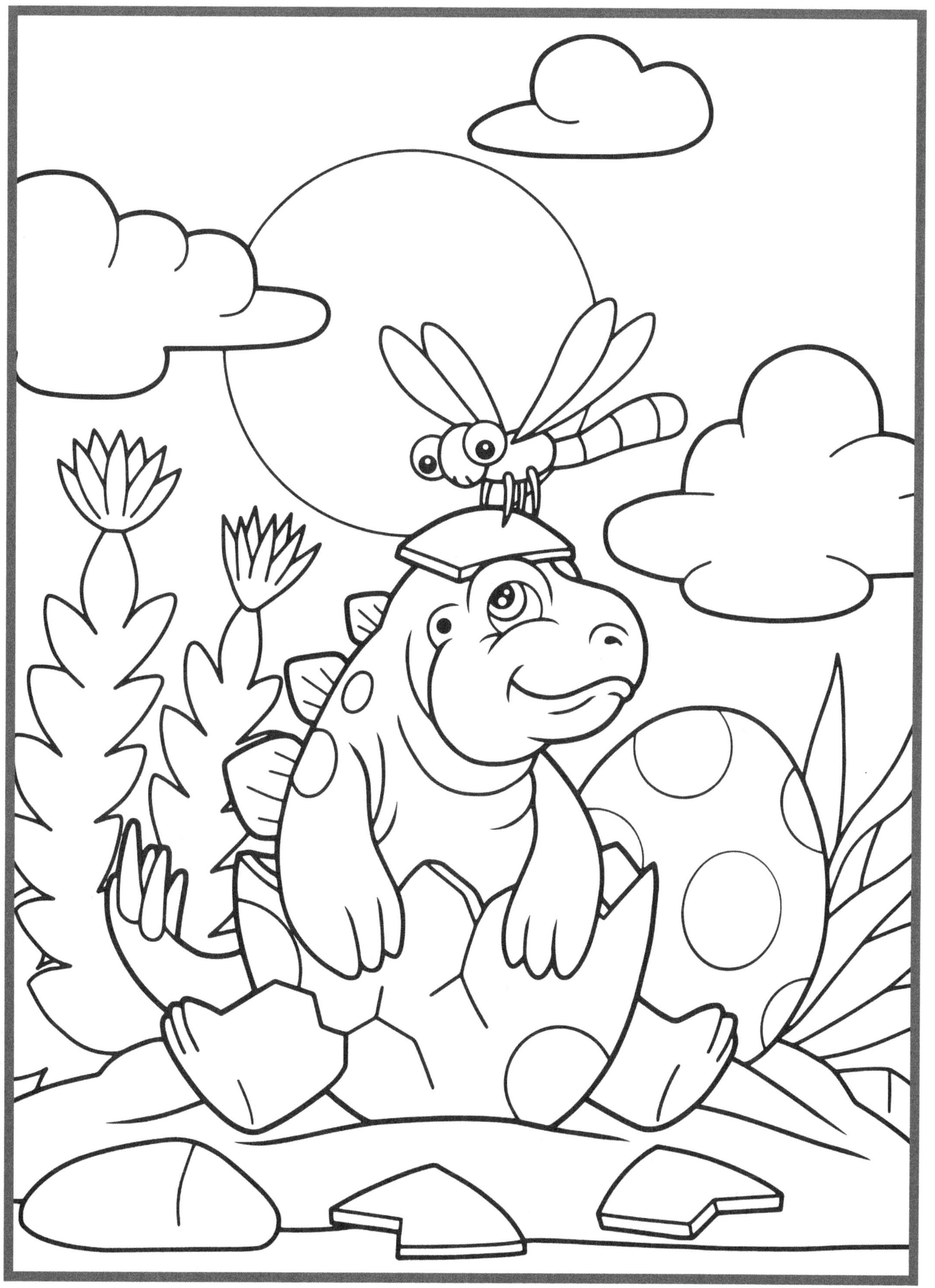

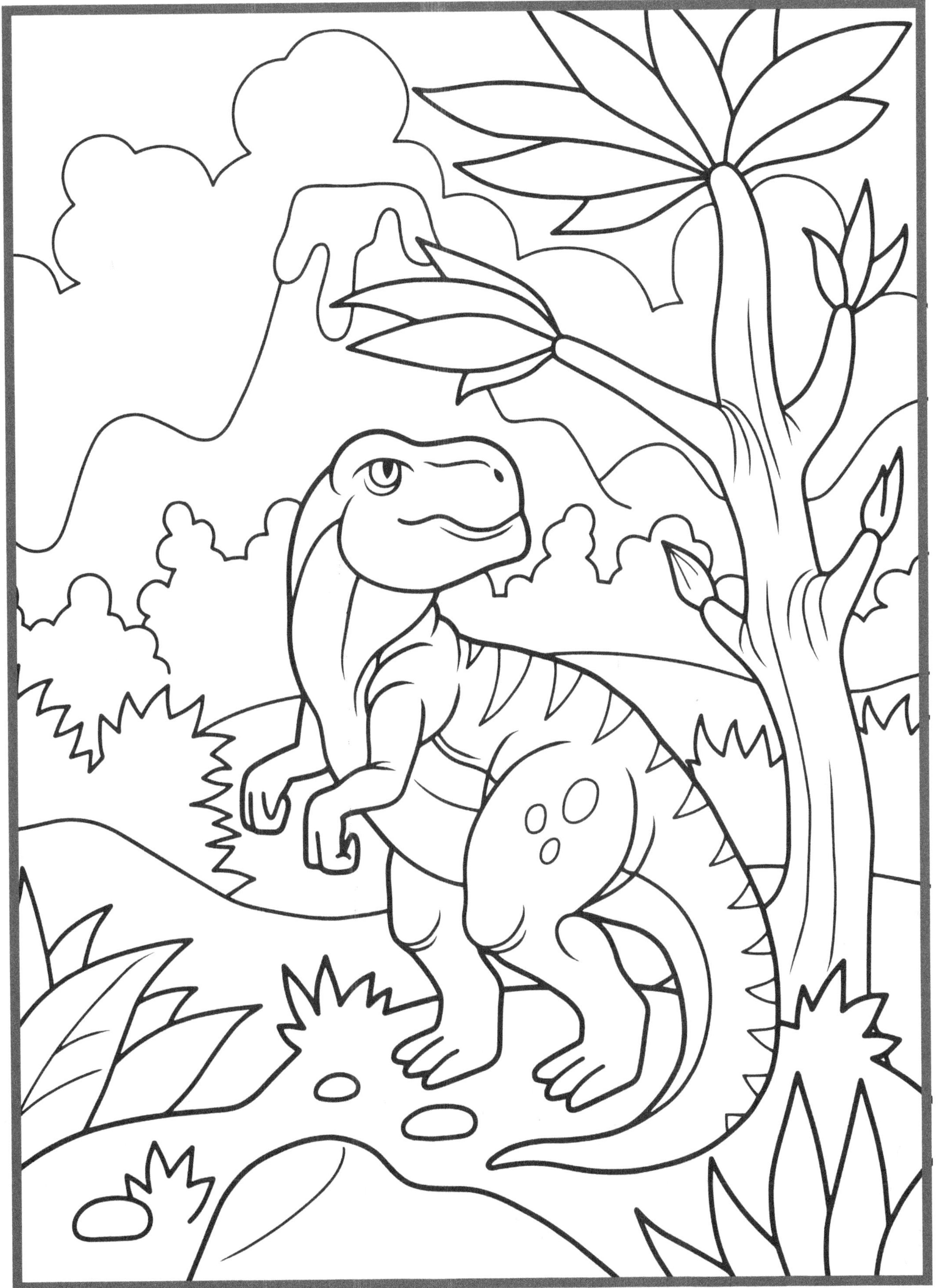

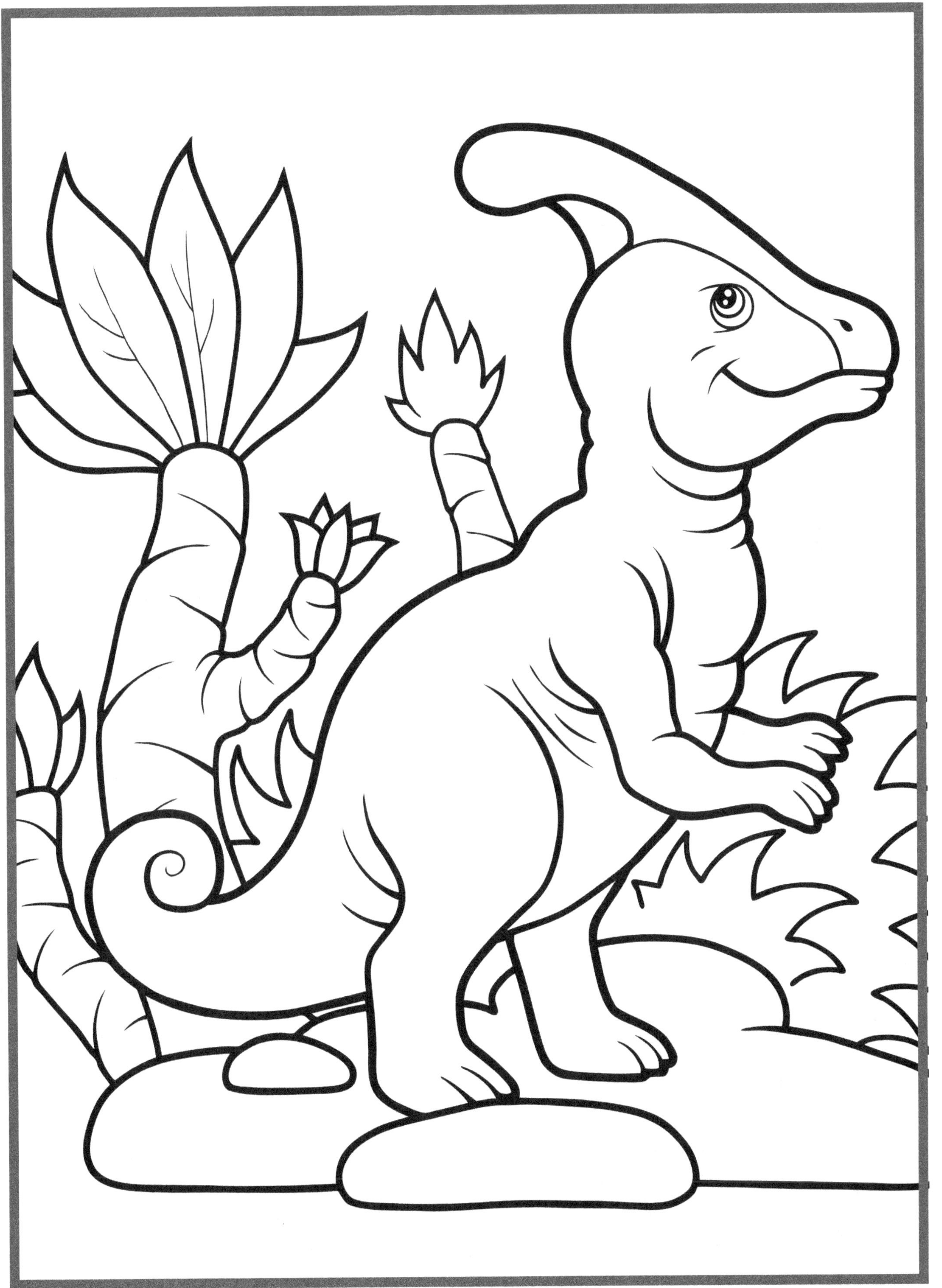

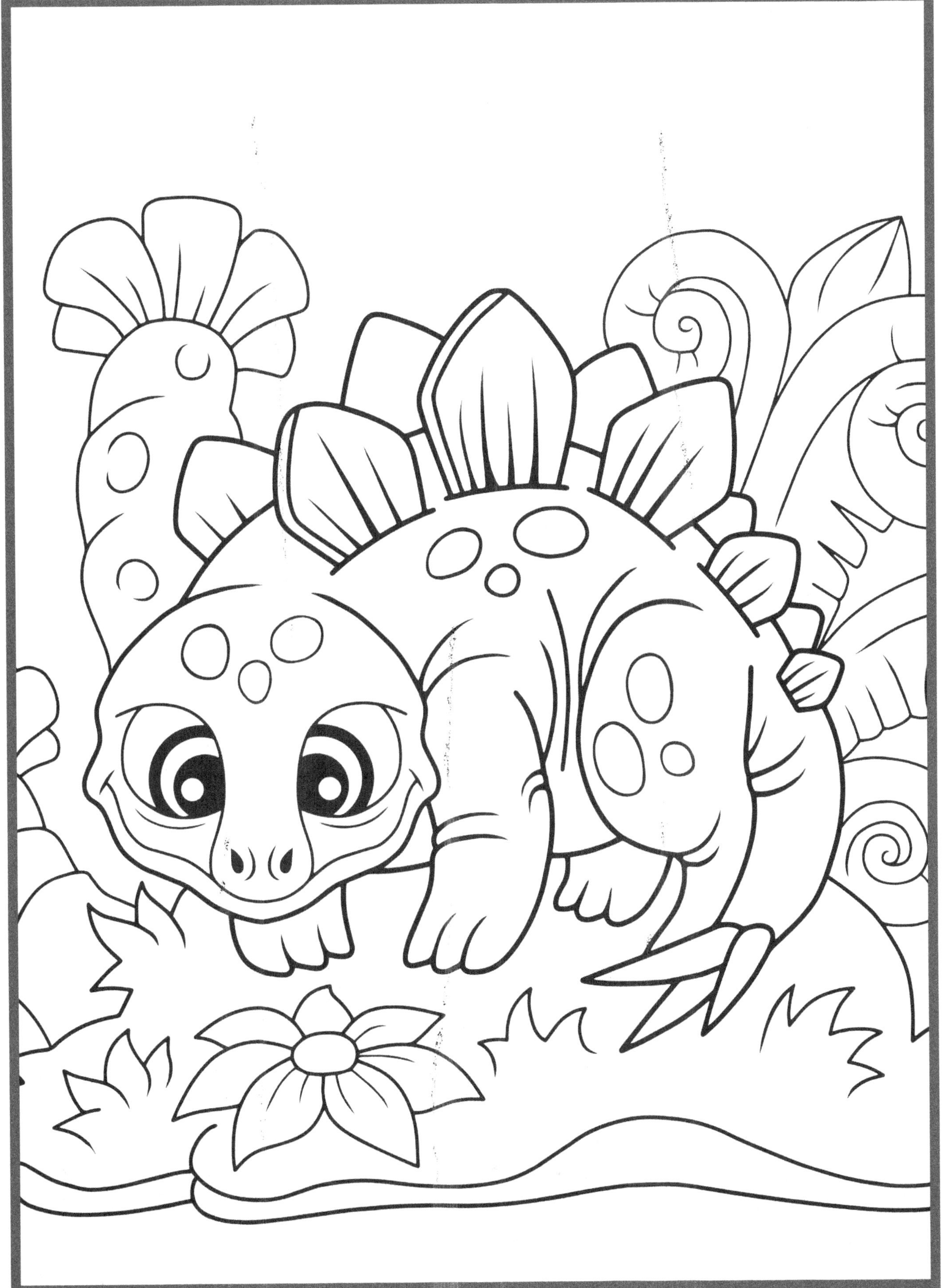

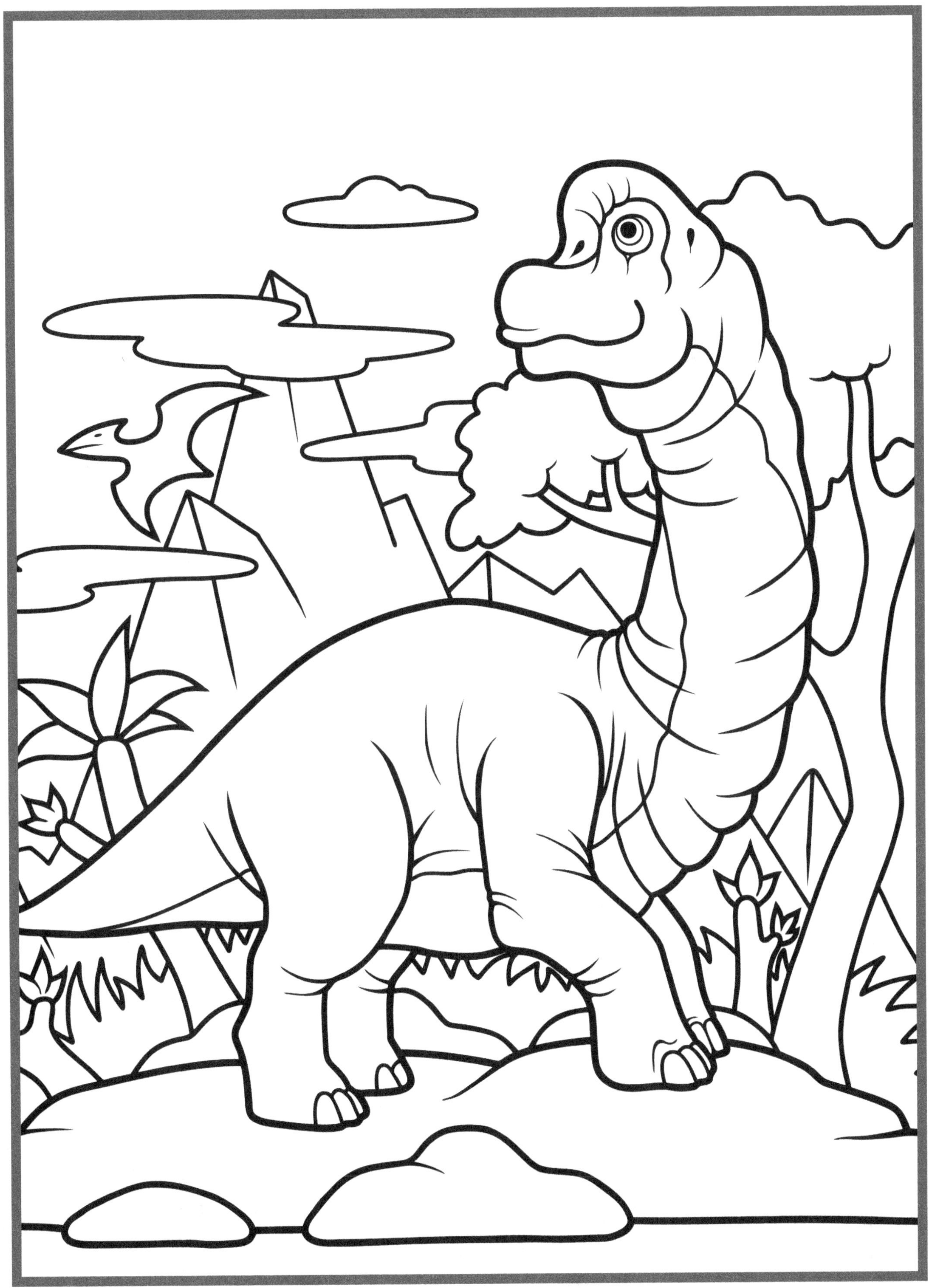

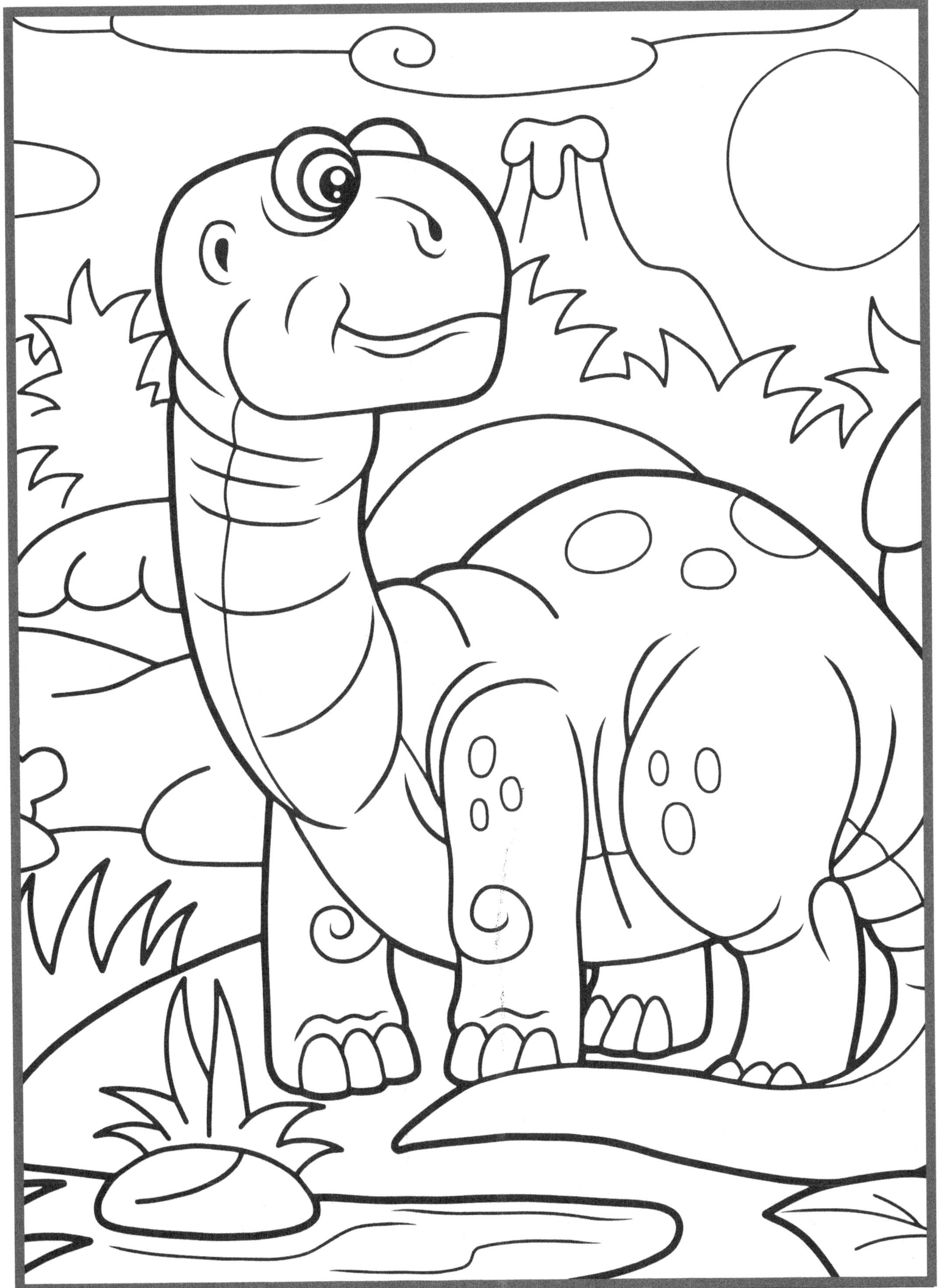

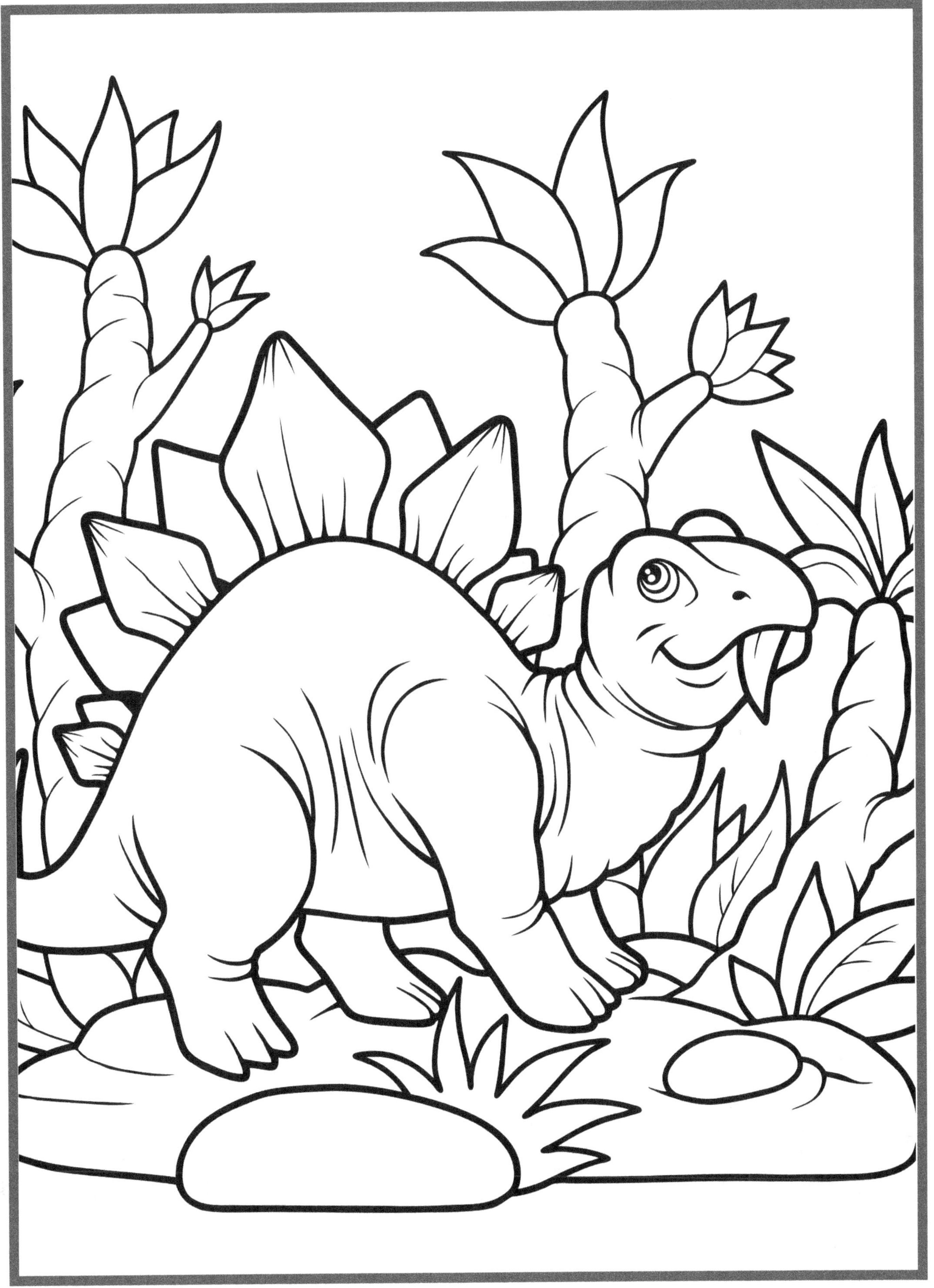

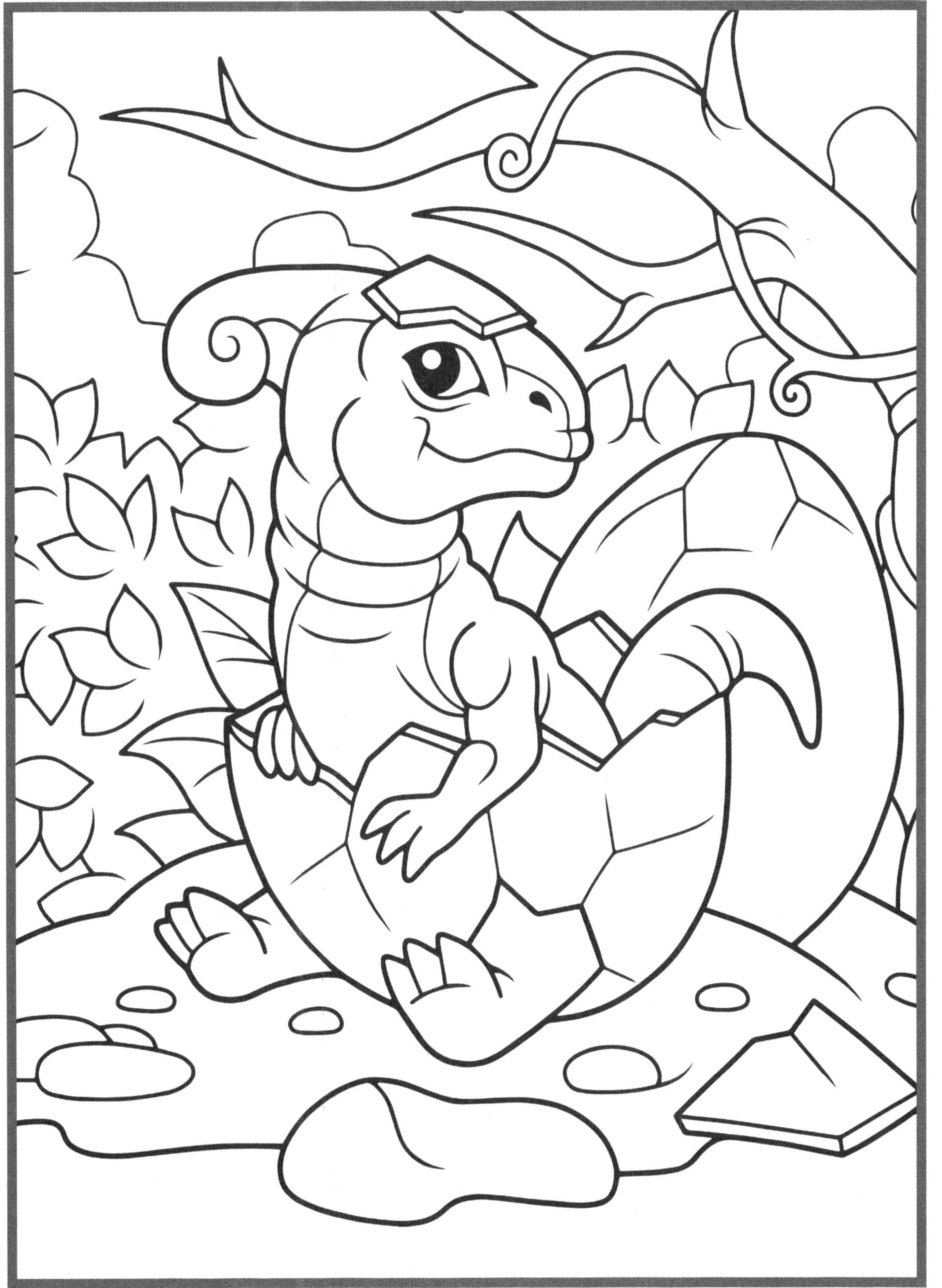

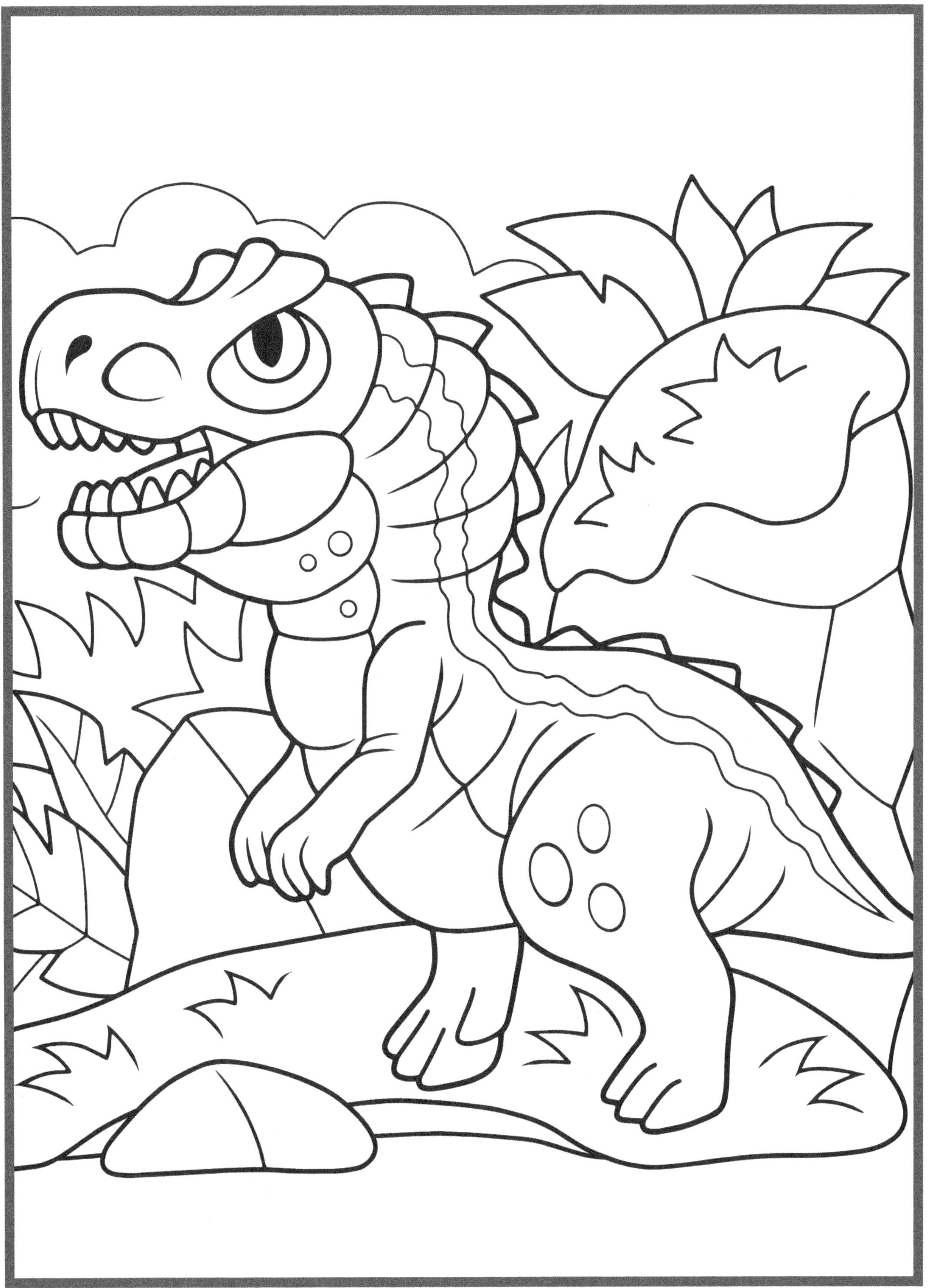

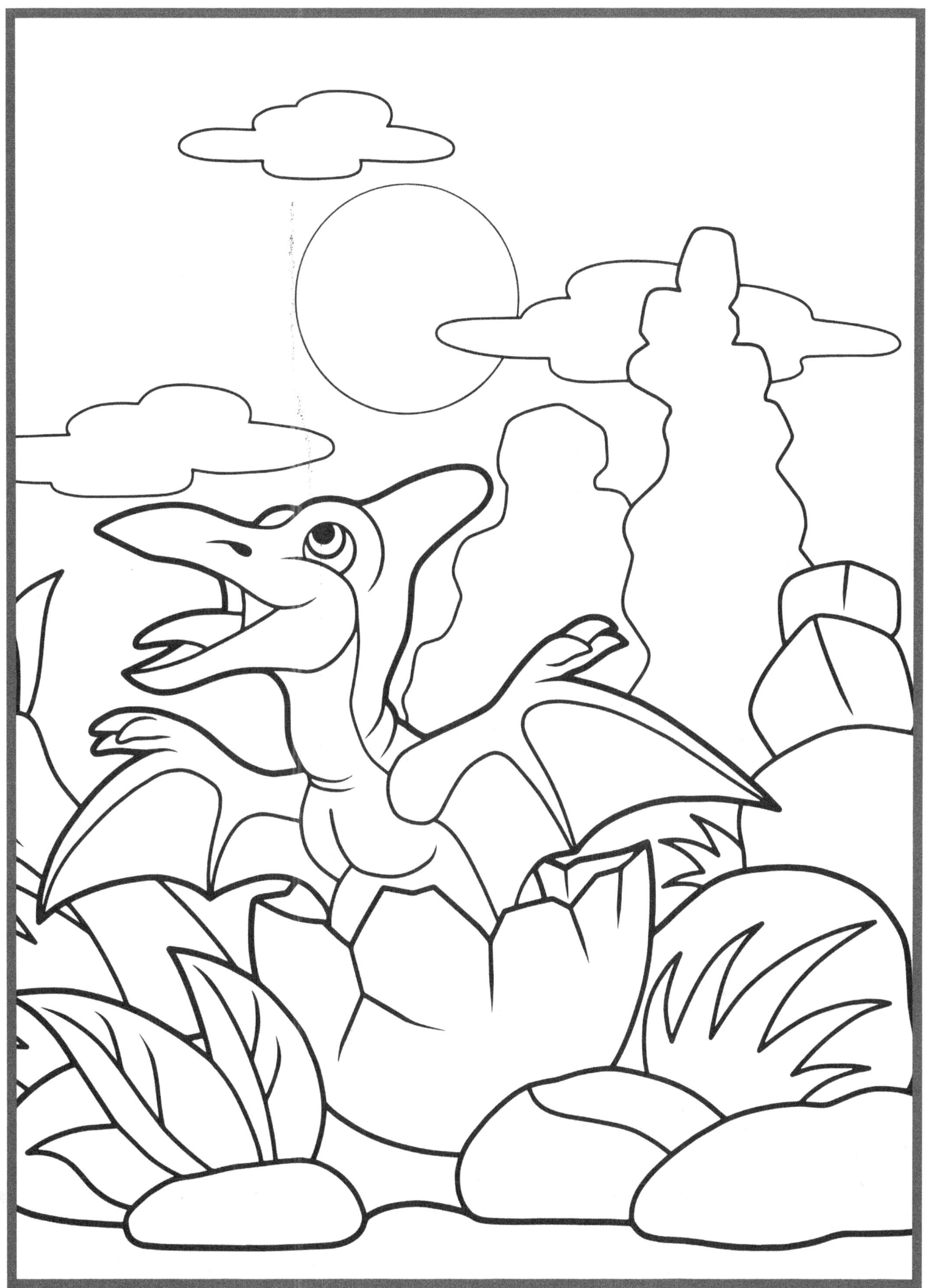

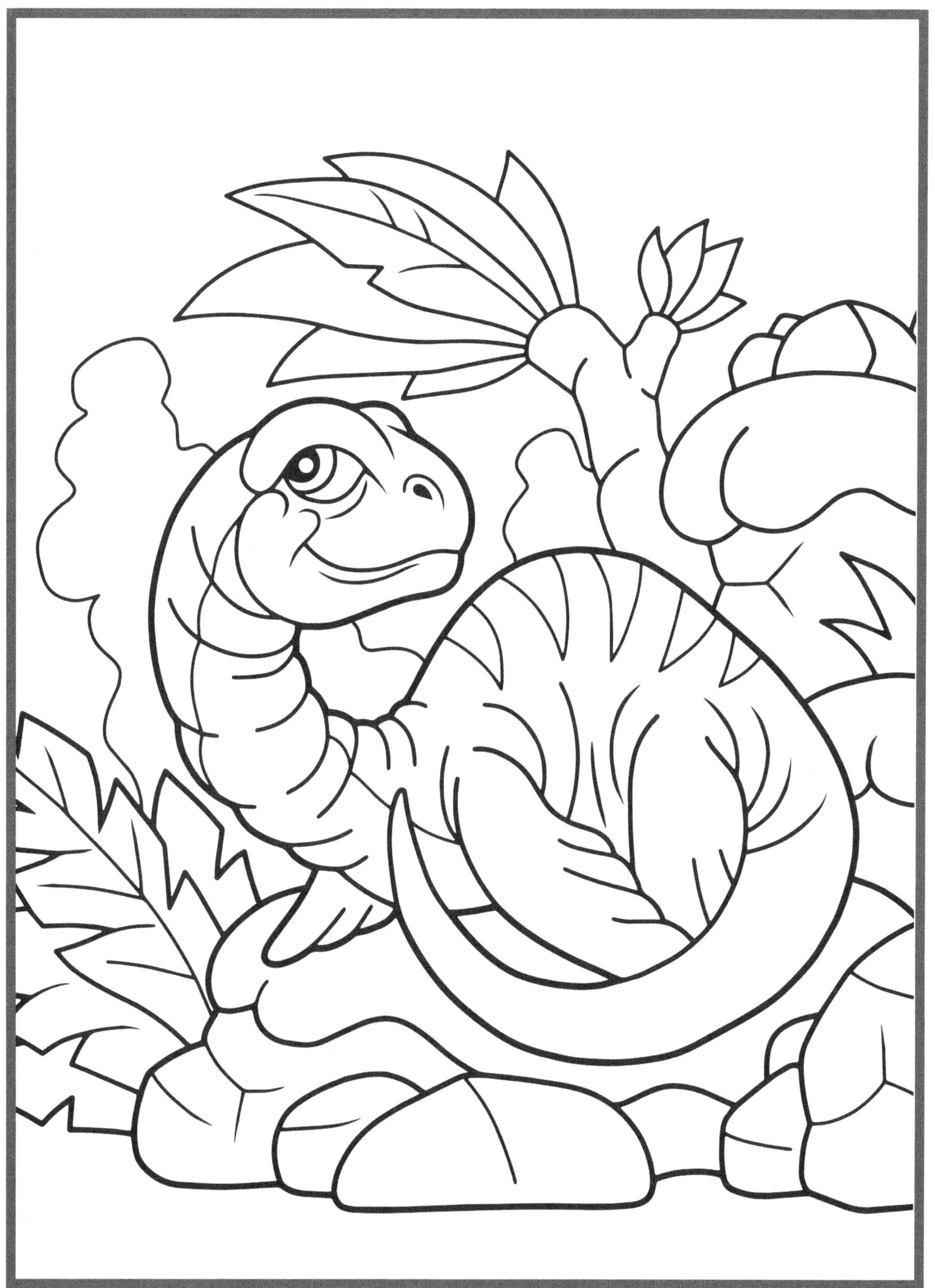

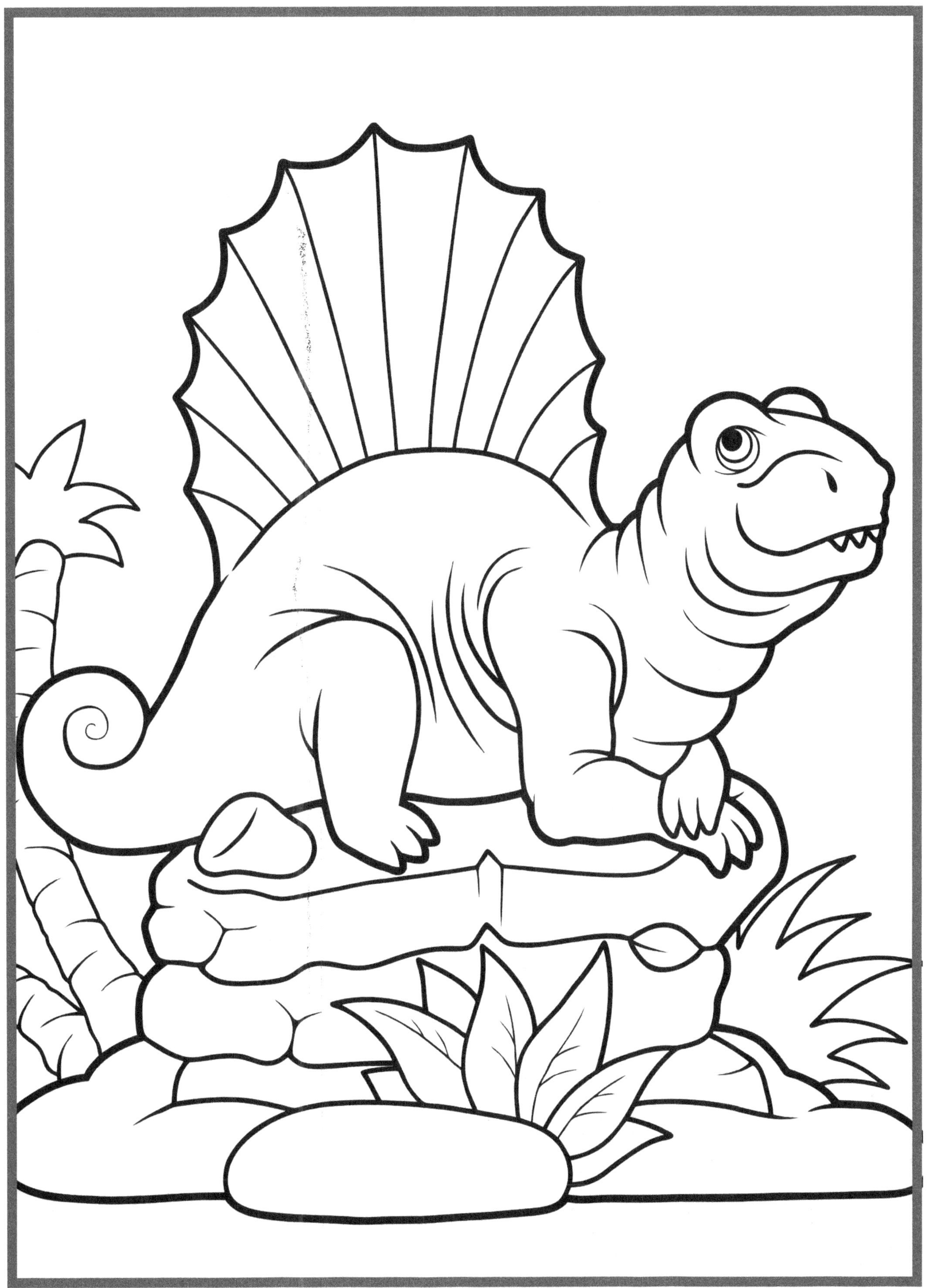

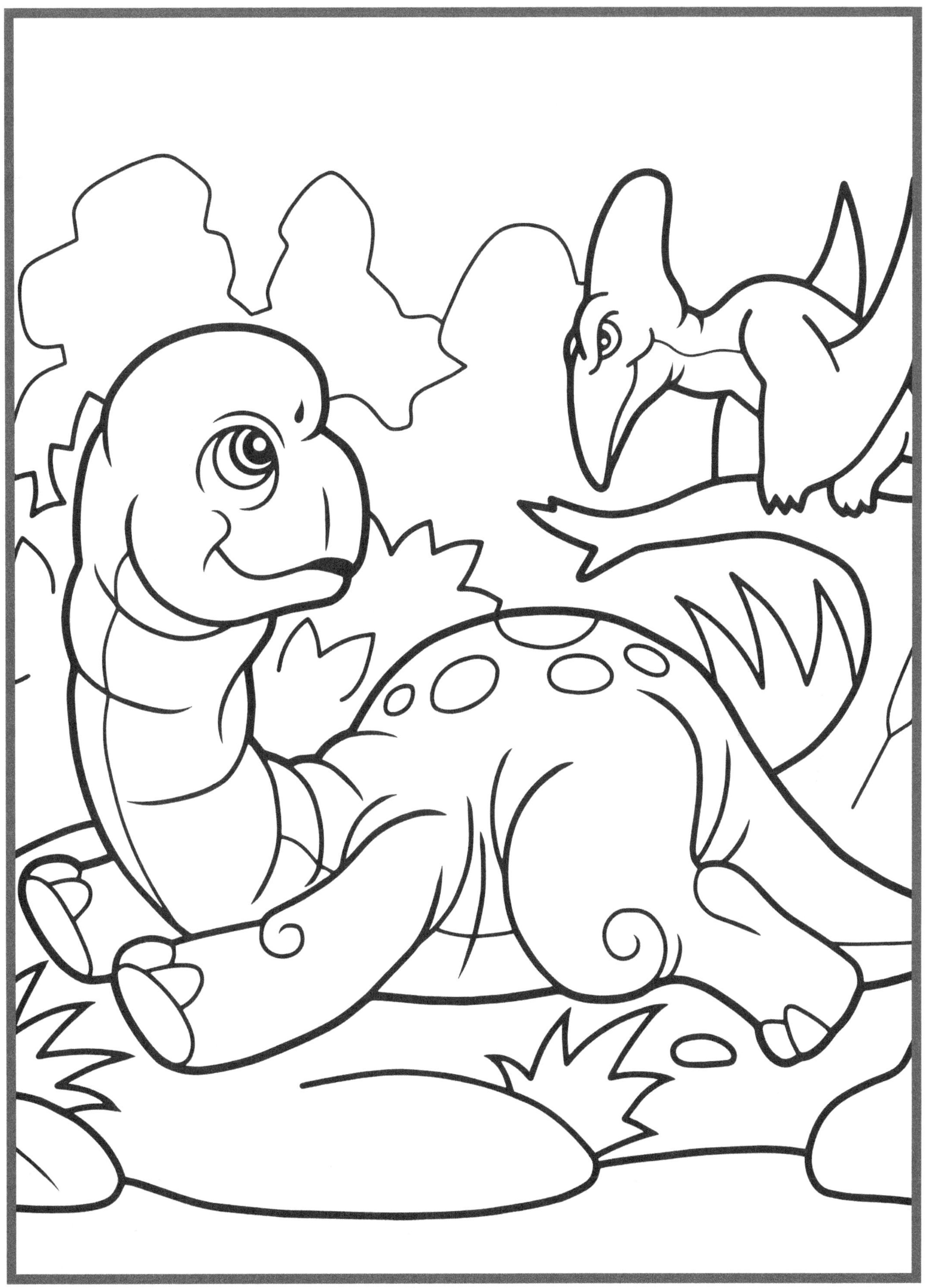

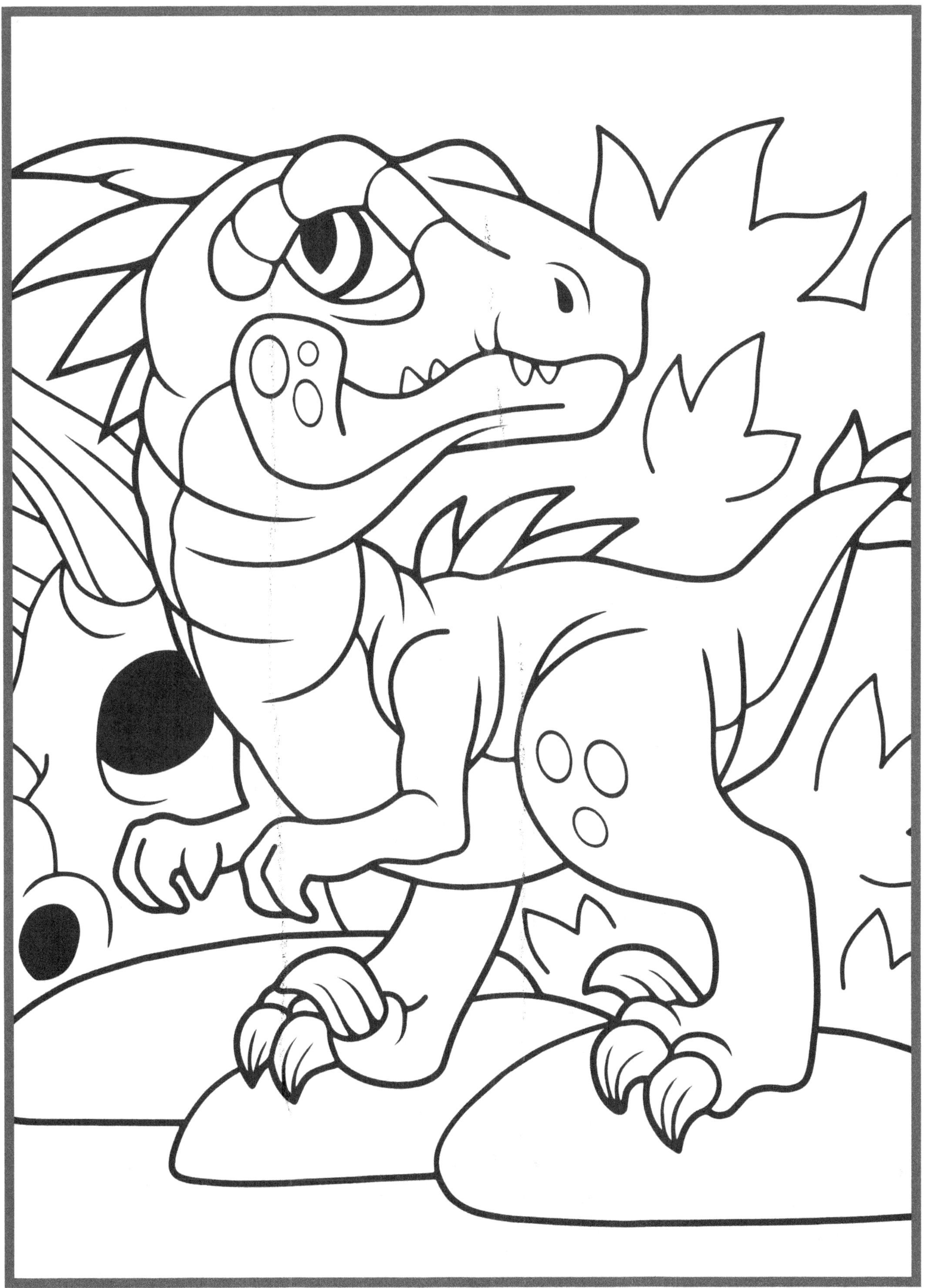

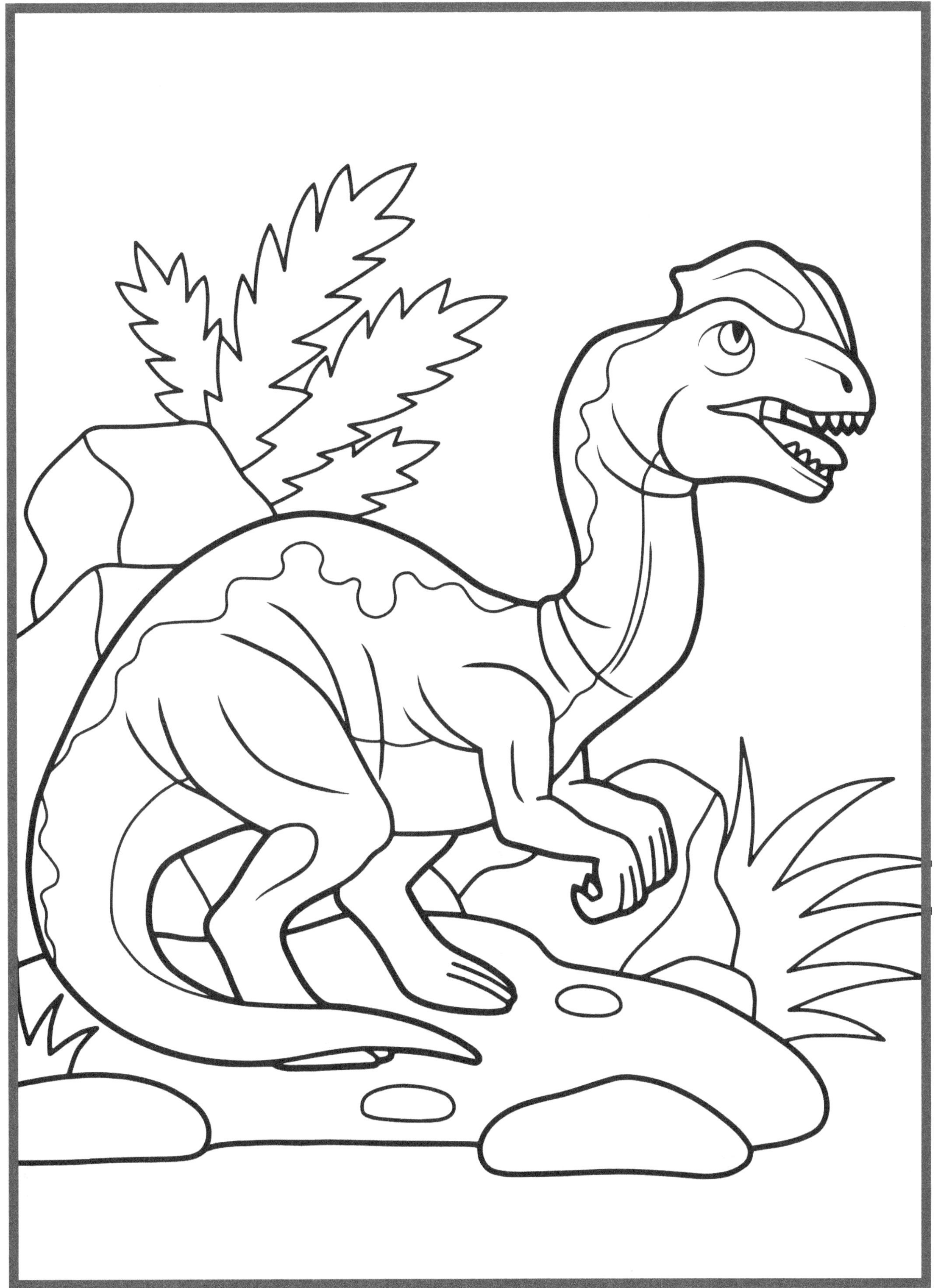

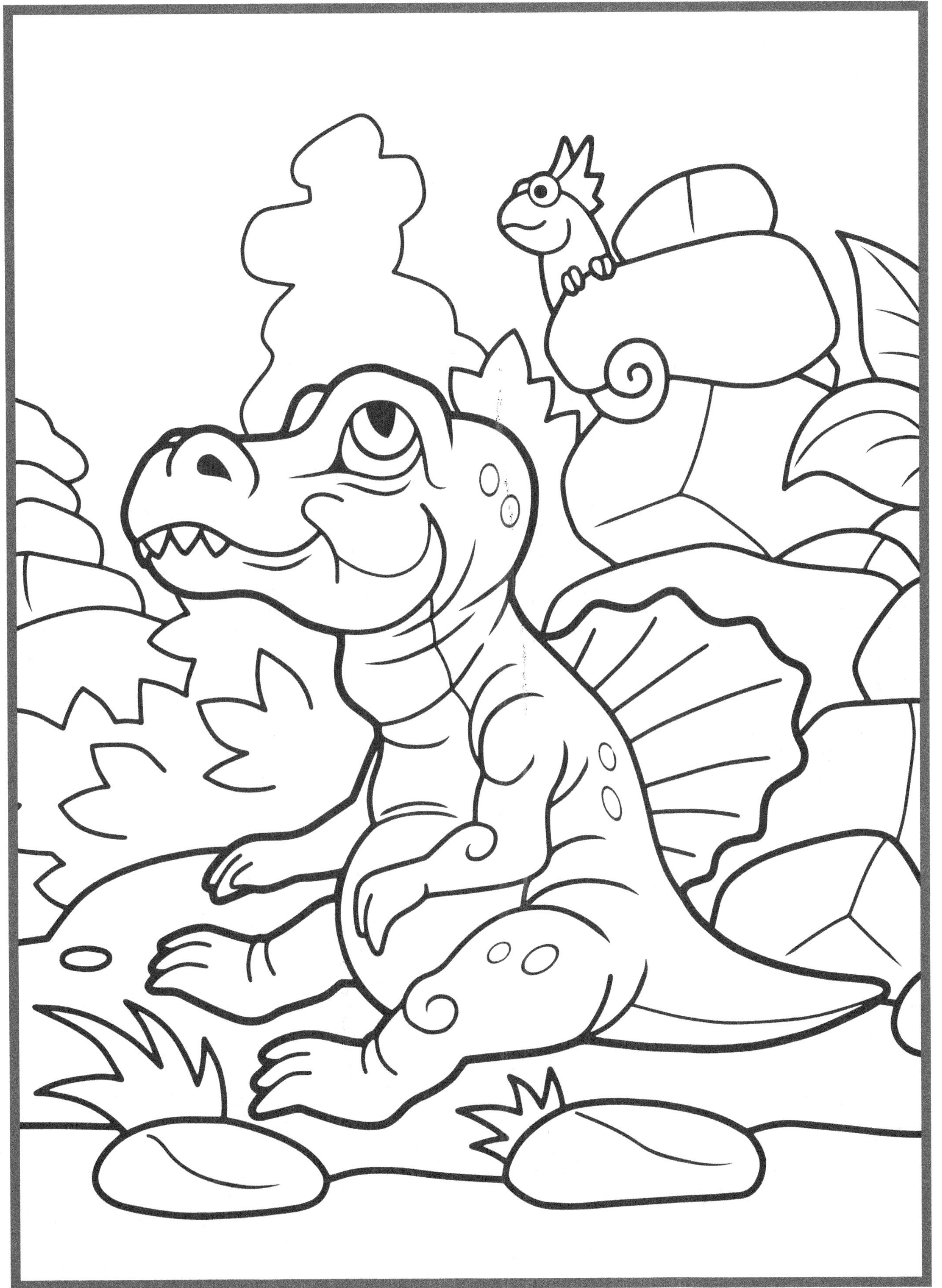

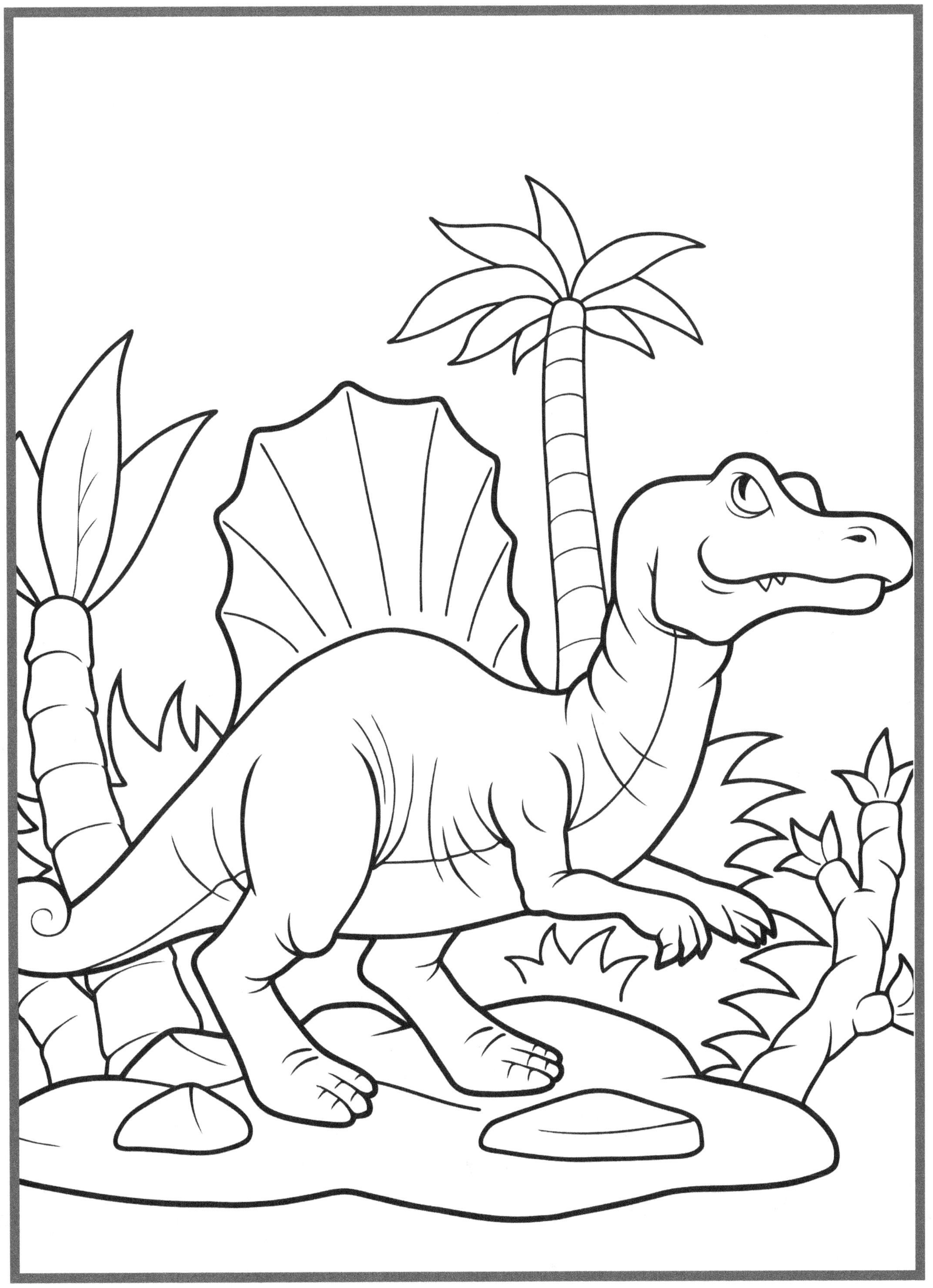

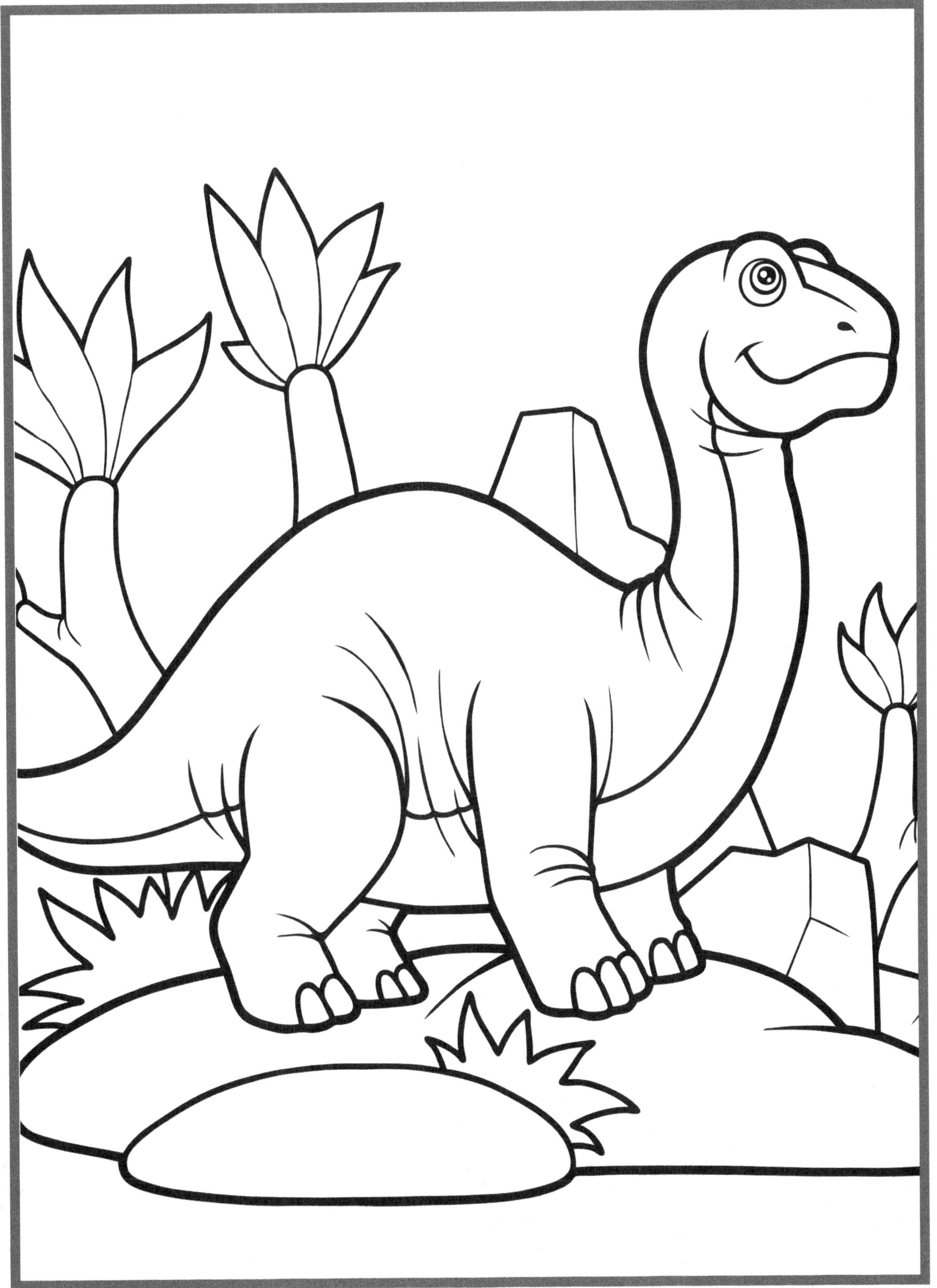

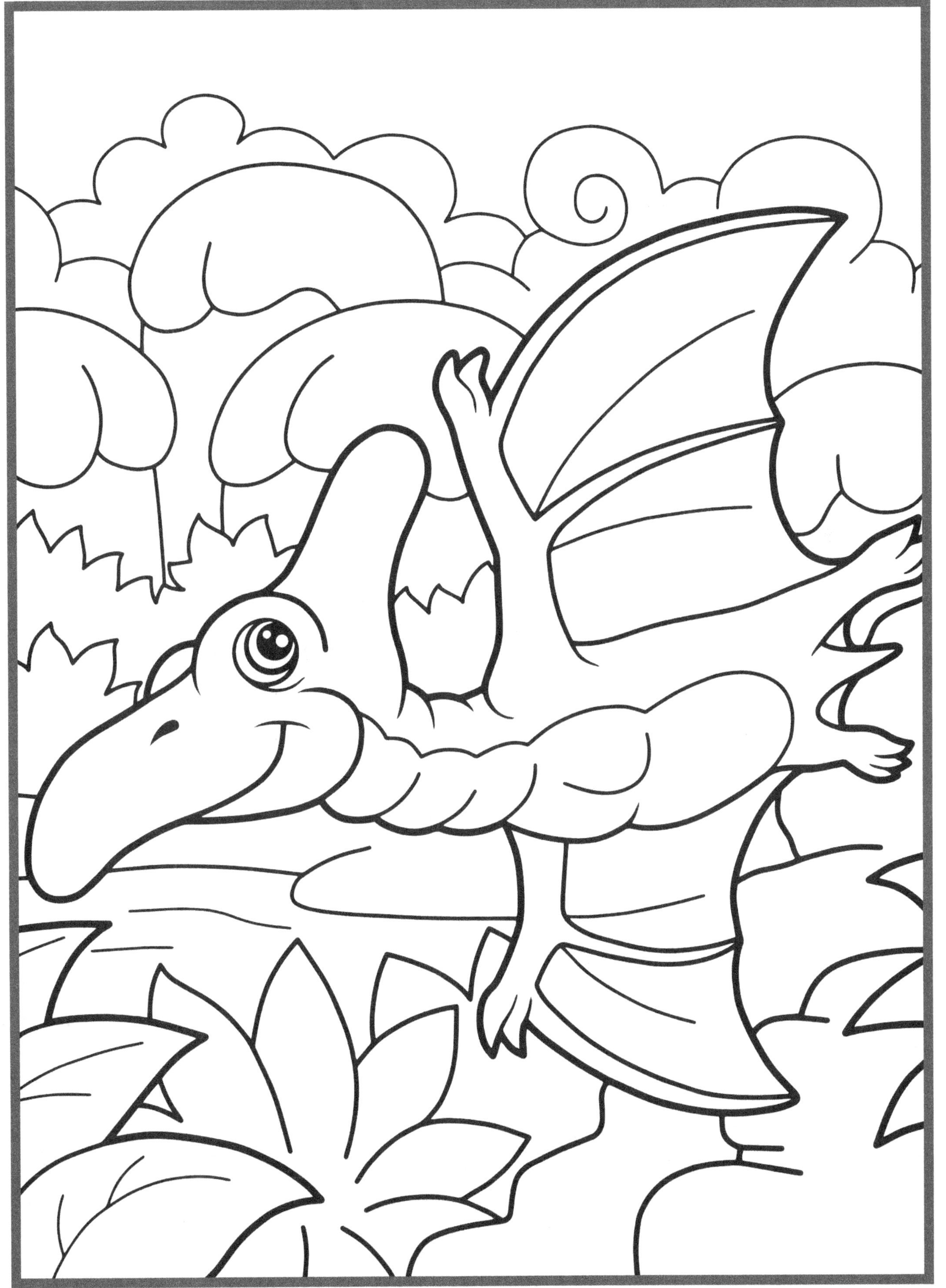

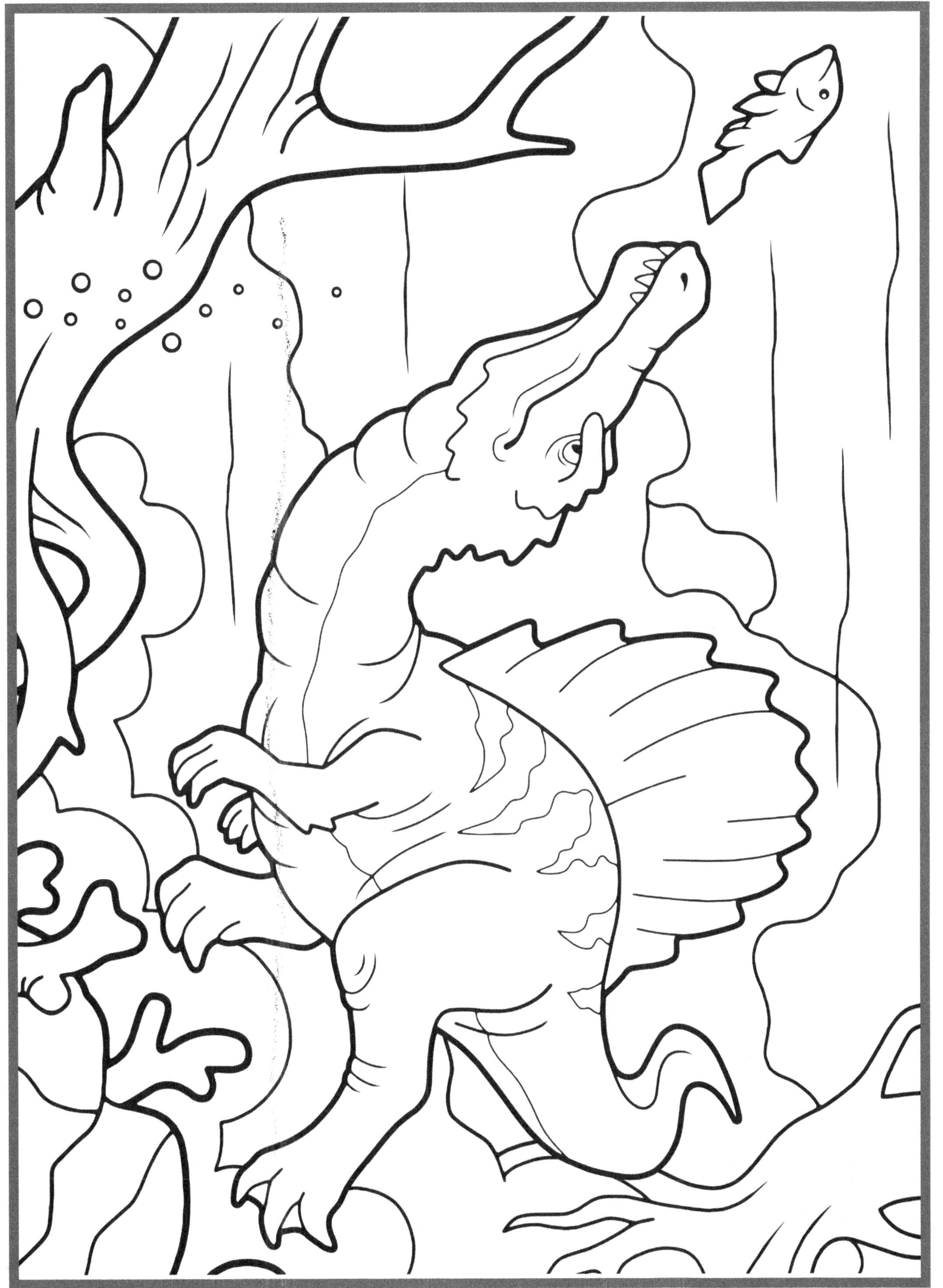

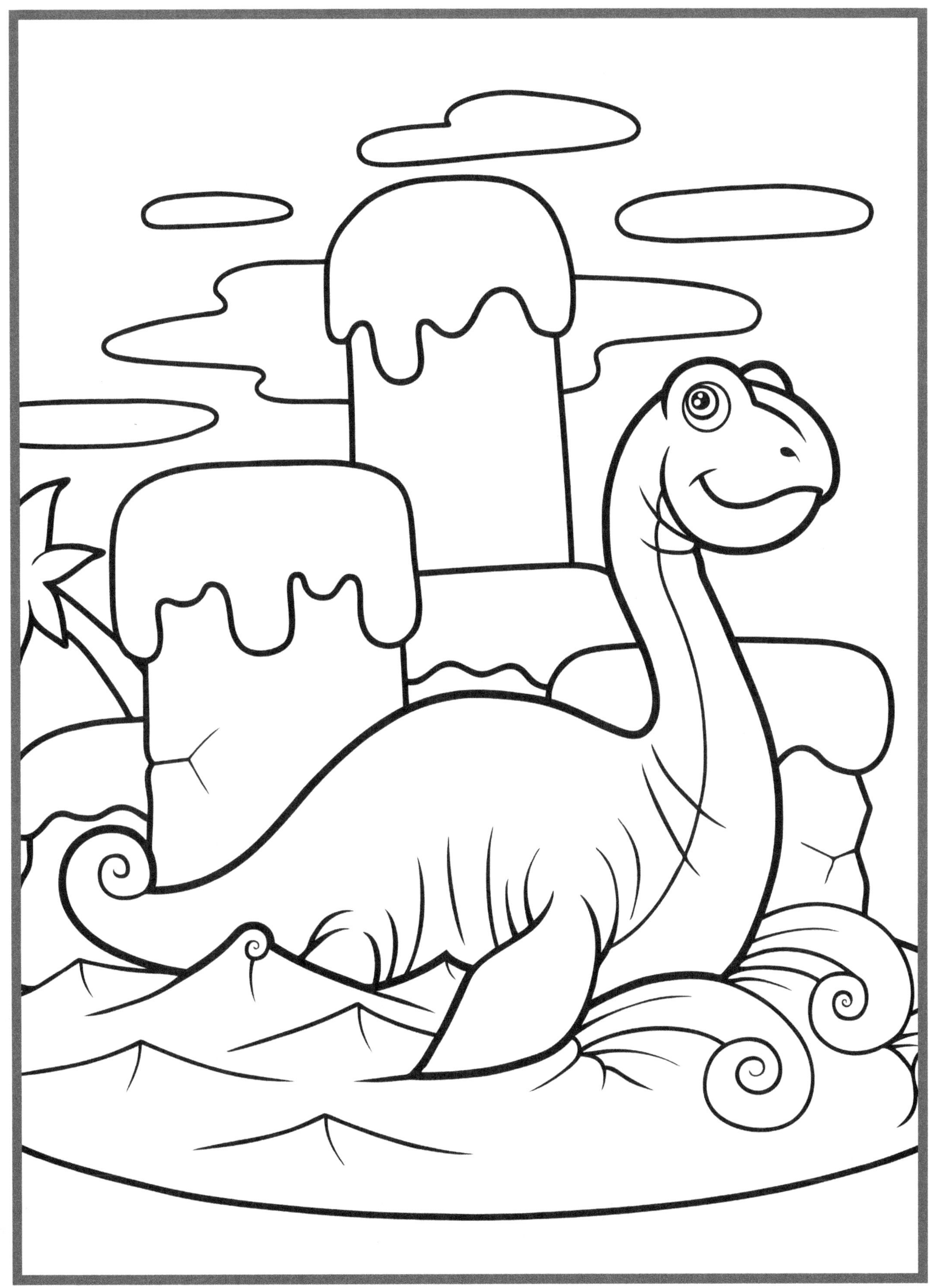

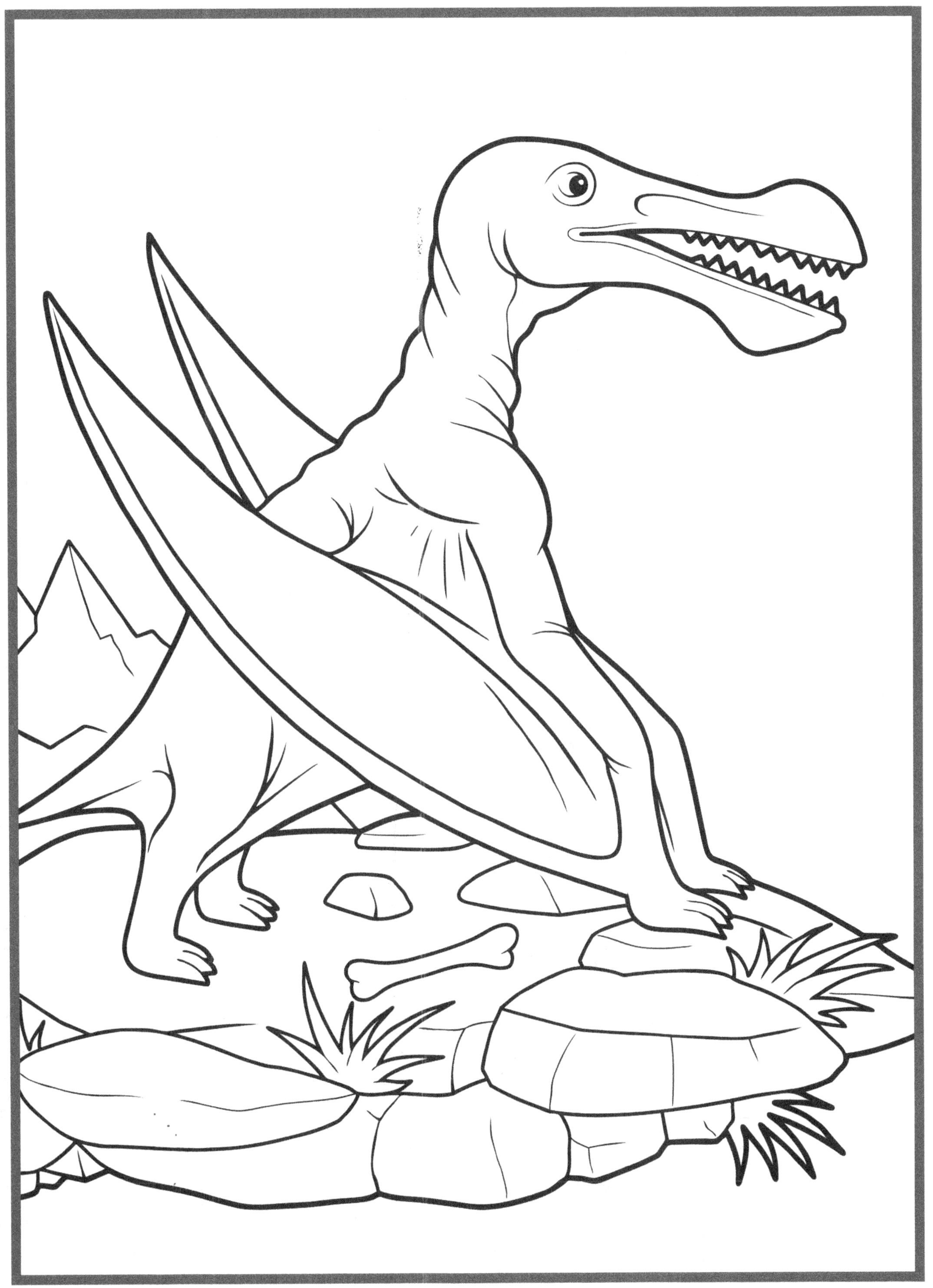

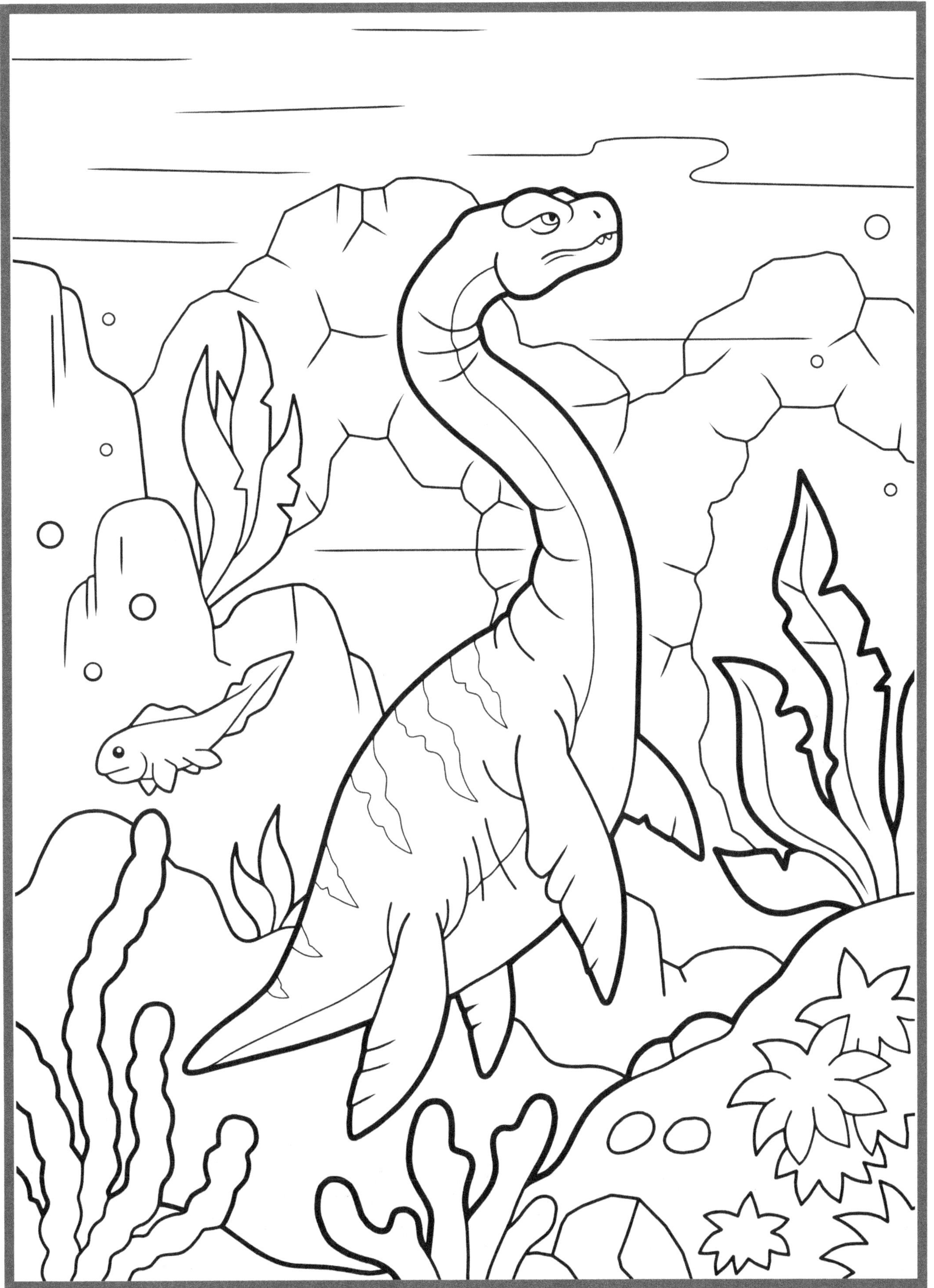

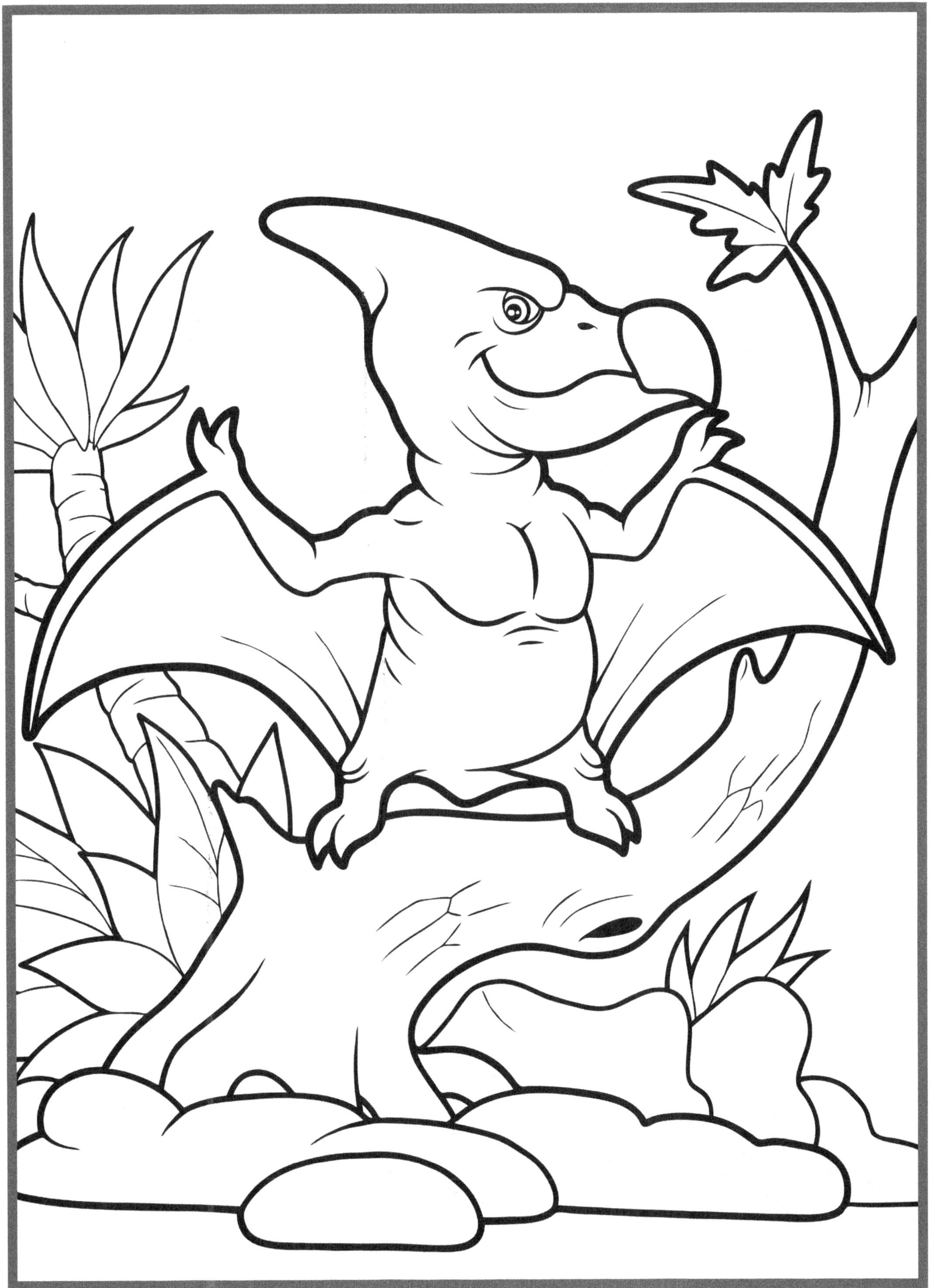

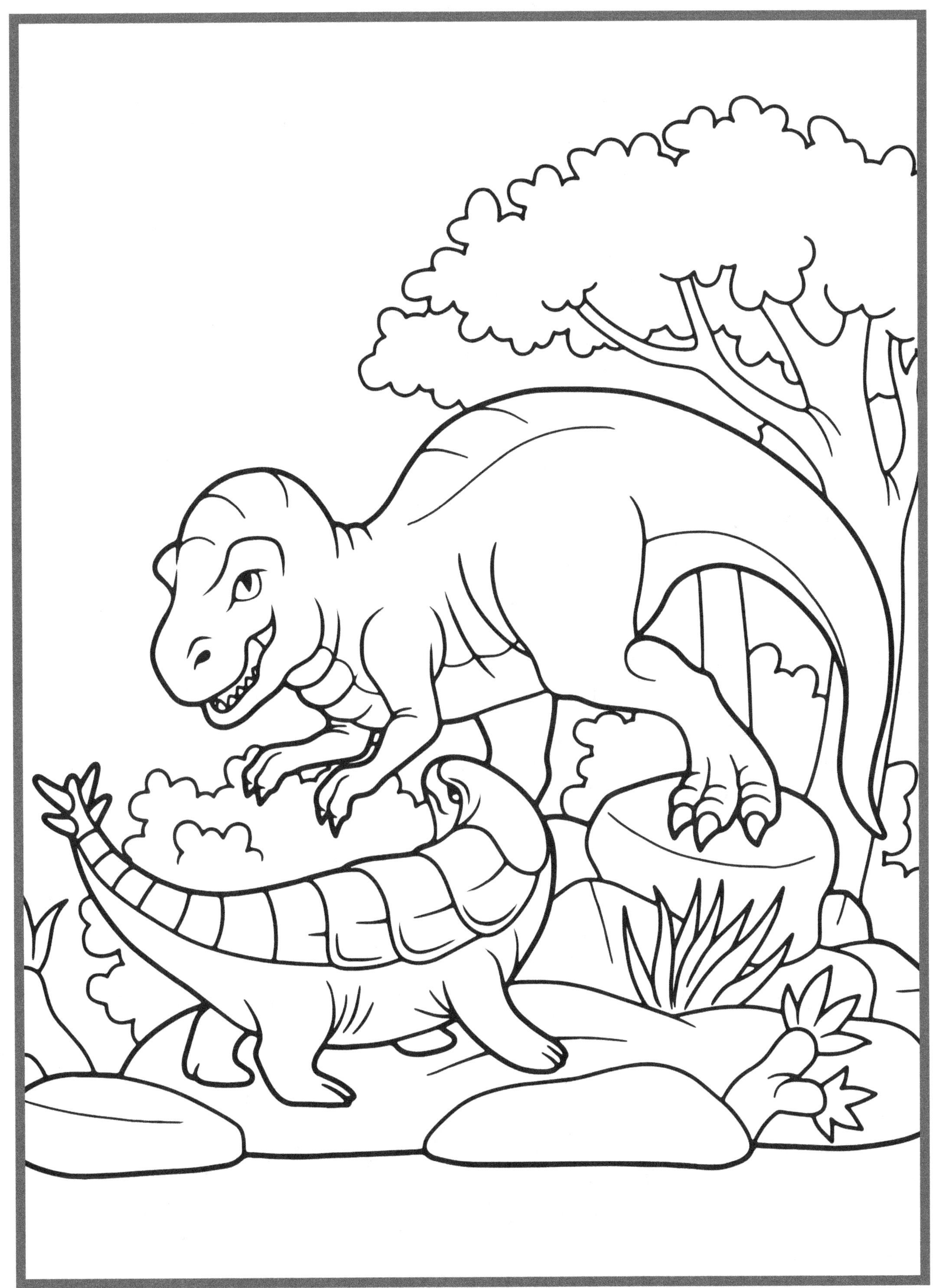

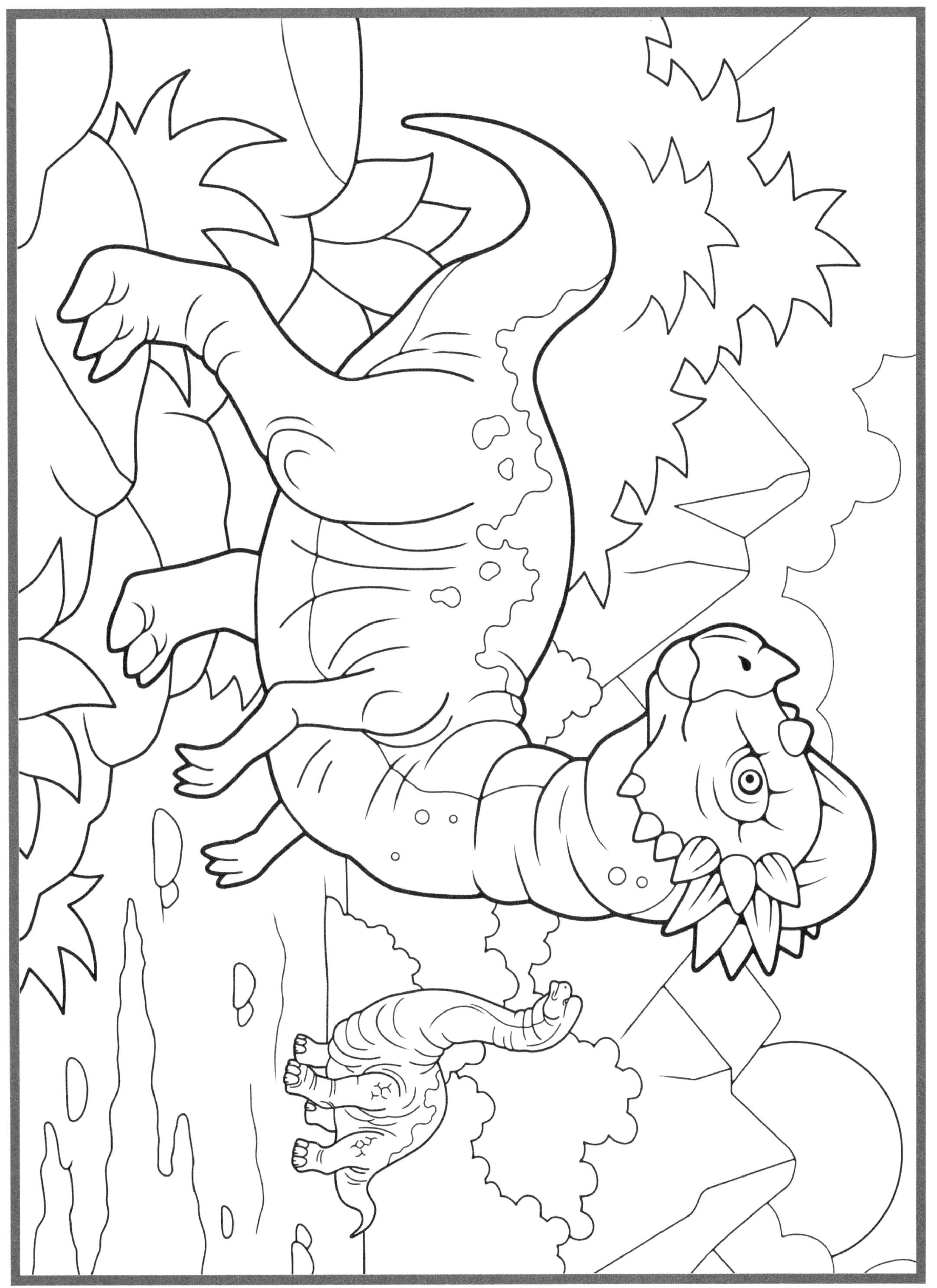